# THE MANAGER

## RON ATKINSON

# THE MANAGER

## RON ATKINSON

In collaboration with Tim Rich

deCoubertin
BOOKS

First published as a hardback by deCoubertin Books Ltd in 2016.
Softback edition published 2017.

deCoubertin Books, Studio I, Baltic Creative Campus, Liverpool, L1 OAH
www.decoubertin.co.uk

ISBN: 978-1-909245-55-6

Cover design by Leslie Priestley.

Typeset by Sabahat Muhammed.

Printed and bound by Standart.

*I would like to dedicate this memoir to all the many decent people in football and in broadcasting who have helped me to understand the game a little better.*

# CONTENTS

# ACKNOWLEDGEMENTS

I'D LIKE TO ACKNOWLEDGE ALL THE HELP GIVEN TO ME THROUGH-
out my career by so many people and for the love and support of my wife, Maggie,
and our family. I would like to thank the publishers, DeCoubertin for engaging
me to write my memoirs and to Tim Rich for directing the book and putting my
thoughts on to paper.

Best wishes

Ron Atkinson,
July 2016

# ONE

THEY WERE ALIENS. NOT THE ALIENS WE WOULD READ ABOUT in the comic books of the 1950s but in their long leather coats they seemed to come from another world. They looked like gods.

It was December 1954; I was fifteen, a ground-staff boy at Wolverhampton Wanderers watching Honved's players walk out on to the pitch, a pitch that I and the rest of the Wolves staff had done our best to turn into a bog. I can still see Ferenc Puskas walking through the rain and the Molineux floodlights.

In theory it was a friendly but nobody was treating it as such. Wolves were the champions of England, Honved were the champions of Hungary. When Wolves came back from two goals down to win the *Daily Mail* carried a headline that proclaimed 'Hail Wolves, Champions of the World'. It was the game that inspired the European Cup.

We knew many of that Honved team had been the core of the Hungary side that had put six past England at Wembley and then scored seven against them in Budapest. We were standing in a little enclosure at Molineux called the Players' Pen. Wolves ran out in what they called their 'Floodlit Kit' with big, billowing, luminous shirts. Then on came Honved in white shirts with two thin red hoops. The shirts were tight, everything about them was tight.

They were two up in minutes. And then our work began to tell. It had been pouring down over the Midlands but the Wolves manager, Stan Cullis, had ordered the pitch soaked. We stood in the rain, hosing it and then rolling it. The *Daily Mail* said it resembled the surface of a four-day-old cattle show.

As the rain came down, the Hungarians couldn't cope. Puskas tried his trademark drag-back and the ball became trapped in the mud. They literally became bogged down. Wolves, who ought to have been beaten by six, won 3–2.

Cullis had intended to use more than just ground-staff boys with hoses to beat the Hungarians. Wolves employed an analyst called Wing Commander Charles Reep, who argued that most goals resulted from three passes.

It formed the basis of the theories that Graham Taylor was to use so successfully at Watford. Reep dominated Molineux to the extent that, if you played a square pass in your own half of the pitch, there would be trouble. If Stan Cullis saw it, he would go absolutely barmy.

Cullis believed in the power game but Wolves were not as crude as Wimbledon were to become, and in Peter Broadbent they had one of the best footballers England ever produced. Cullis was, nevertheless, very anxious to prove to us that the Hungarian way was not the way football should be played.

Before the game, Cullis took us all into the Molineux Hotel at the top of the ground to watch a film of the Hungarians beating England 6–3 at Wembley the year before. We analysed the first goal: Hungary score almost straight from the kick-off. There are half-a-dozen passes, Jimmy Dickinson tries to get his toe-end on to one of them, and turns it into a square pass. The ball is then played out to Nandor Hidegkuti, who whacks it in the net. Cullis turns round and says, 'There you go, three passes.' Through my teenage eyes it looked like fifteen passes but, naturally, nobody in that room had the courage to say so.

Cullis never received the recognition he deserved. He won the championship three times and the FA Cup twice. The irony was that he was a classic ball-playing centre-half who when he became a manager emphasised power and drive, but he ruled with a rod of iron. The only person I ever saw stand up to him when I was on the staff at Wolves was Peter Broadbent. Even the internationals like Billy Wright were in absolute awe of him.

Broadbent was a fantastic footballer who had a body-swerve you wouldn't believe, and one day Cullis had a go because he wasn't tracking back and Peter just let him have it. He knew he was a player and he didn't need to be told how to play.

While the names of Busby and Shankly resonate across football, Stan Cullis's reputation disappeared outside the Black Country. Wolves sacked him very messily in 1964 and when he reappeared at Birmingham something was missing, something had gone. He never achieved anything much at St Andrew's and when he left Birmingham, he left the game completely.

But he was a visionary. The floodlit games Wolves staged against Honved, Spartak Moscow and Moscow Dynamo changed everything. It sparked an idea. It was the first time any of us had seen foreign footballers up close, and Puskas and Kocsis would be among the greats, worthy of inclusion in any World XIs you could name. After the Hungarian Revolution in 1956 they were scattered throughout Europe. Kocsis and Czibor went to Barcelona, Puskas to Real Madrid, where he scored hat-tricks in two European Cup finals and managed to be on the losing side in one of them.

Foreign footballers are everywhere and the Premier League has far too many mediocre ones. What was once exotic and special has become mundane and ordinary. The argument is that they are cheaper than British footballers but I wonder how true that is. The Premier League argues that it is the best in the world but how many overseas players who have come here can be said to have been truly great?

Gianfranco Zola might have been the very best. Sergio Aguero is probably the best finisher, perhaps just ahead of Ruud van Nistelrooy. People talk about Dennis Bergkamp but Alex Ferguson never really rated him. Fergie's argument was always that Bergkamp seldom produced in the big games, and my memory of Bergkamp is clouded by one match. In September 1994, Aston Villa played Inter Milan in the UEFA Cup and Bergkamp was hopeless, anaemic. If I flick though the games where I stood on the touchline and watched him take on one of my teams, I cannot remember a game in which he shone.

Roy Keane said that he could not remember a single European game Eric Cantona turned. I remember watching him at Stuttgart in the European Cup when he had just started for Leeds. He struck a long cross-field ball that was cut out and led to Stuttgart scoring their first goal in a 3–0 win. Leeds won the return at Elland Road 4–1 and were out on away goals. Then they then discovered Stuttgart had fielded an ineligible player and the tie had to be replayed in Barcelona – a game that Leeds won.

But despite his error, watching from the stands in Stuttgart I thought Cantona was an extremely useful player – but not the phenomenon he was to become at Manchester United. When I talked to Gordon Strachan and Gary McAllister about him after that match, they hadn't the time of day for him. They thought Cantona a waster.

And yet though they worshipped him on the training ground at Manchester United, there was an element of waste about Cantona's play in Europe, especially in the Champions League semi-final against Borussia Dortmund in 1997. United had reached the semis despite losing three matches in the group stage, but Dortmund did not seem the strongest opponents and Cantona had chance after chance. He squandered them all.

Thinking of other players, Thierry Henry was phenomenal, Patrick Vieira was magnificent and, though he might have been an acquired taste, I did like David Ginola. Obviously there would have been days when as a manager he would have driven you up the wall but he had a beautiful way of playing. He made his debut for Newcastle when I was managing Coventry and he stretched us until we broke.

Of the foreign footballers I managed, Arnold Muhren and Roland

Nilsson at Manchester United and Sheffield Wednesday were complete professionals. Pierre van Hooijdonk wasn't, while Paolo di Canio was simply mad.

And yet a generation and a half before I began studying Di Canio's body language for clues, there was this sense of wonder that foreign footballers existed at all when as a fourteen-year-old I sat in front of a nine-inch television screen that came complete with a magnifying glass. It was the only one in our street and in November 1953 Hungary were playing England at Wembley. It was the day football changed forever.

The last time I'd been invited in front of that screen was for the 1953 FA Cup final, the Matthews Final.

My dad was a boxer, swimmer and sprinter, who played baseball for a factory team in Birmingham and played football for Ayr United during the war, although he was never a pro.

I remember my dad urging me to go and watch Stanley Matthews because 'this will probably be his last season'. We duly went and he played on for another ten years. He was the world's greatest player, although the world we knew comprised of England, Wales, Ireland and Scotland. We had been beaten in the World Cup by the United States in Belo Horizonte but none of us at Lea Village Secondary School imagined England was not the greatest football nation on the planet.

Matthews was ahead of his time. He was a vegetarian, a teetotaller and he was big on endorsements. He launched a range of boots through the Co-op. The bog-standard one was like an army boot but the deluxe version was beautiful, probably lighter than the modern boot and with a ply fitting that meant you could almost fold them. They were black. The one thing I cannot imagine Stanley Matthews in all his glory doing is playing with one lime-green boot and the other shocking-pink.

It seemed to us that we were the luckiest kids in the world. We grew up in a house in one of the newer council estates on the edge of Birmingham that had what I can only describe as an arena, with a big grassy area on an island in front of the houses.

It was football every day. Even the fathers would come out and play.

Come April, without anybody saying anything, dustbins would be taken out and used as wickets. The only time the games would ever stop was at quarter to seven when somebody's mother would shout that *Dick Barton, Special Agent* was on. You would go in for fifteen minutes, spend the next five talking with your mates about what would happen to Snowy White or whether Jock Anderson could get out of trouble, and then the games would resume.

I was born in Liverpool, my mum's city, and although I was only a few days old when we went back to the Midlands, I tended to spend the summer holidays there. My uncle had a dairy in Goodison Road, on the corner of Peter Road, and when I was a teenager I would help him deliver the milk, pulling a handcart.

The highlights would be putting bottles on the doorsteps of Tommy Jones and Tony McNamara, who played for Everton, and delivering to Michael Holliday, a singer who was briefly known as the 'British Bing Crosby'.

To be a professional footballer was the great dream. The standard of school football was pretty good and the teachers would encourage you – one of my old schoolmasters still umpires in our village. My heroes were Billy Wright, above all Duncan Edwards, and Albert Quixall, who played on the wing for Sheffield Wednesday and Manchester United. British footballers were of course the best in the world. It was so obvious it was never discussed.

And then we all gathered round the nine-inch telly for the second big sporting event of 1953, the one that was billed as 'The Game of the Century', the one between England and Hungary.

What amazed us was that at the kick-off Puskas flicked the ball up and caught it on his instep, and we all turned to each other to say, 'What the hell was that?' Any footballer now could do it; any silly centre-half could probably do it. Then, it was extraordinary.

Hidegkuti scored from the kick-off and what stuck in all our minds was the third Hungarian goal, Puskas dragging the ball back with the sole of his boot as Billy Wright came in to tackle him. Billy went crashing into empty space and he remarked afterwards that he needed a ticket to get back in the ground.

That thrashing was thought then and is still thought now to have been inflicted by a team whose tactics came from nowhere, and yet the FA ought to have had an inkling of what was to come.

There was a coach from Clitheroe called Jimmy Hogan, whom the Hungarian players called Uncle Jimmy. Their manager, Gusztav Sebes, when asked how they had beaten England, replied that Hungary had simply played the football Jimmy Hogan had taught them.

Hogan had managed Aston Villa before the war but he had made his name coaching in Austria, Switzerland and Hungary; later in his career he had been brought back by Villa to coach the kids – and, having left Wolves for Villa, I was one of them.

Aston Villa ran seven teams in those days and Hogan was put in charge of the A team, which was composed of 17–21-year-olds with the odd senior player. I often think that, when people talk of tactics, there is very little that is new in the game and his sessions were astonishingly modern. All the training was done running with a ball.

We played in the Birmingham League, which was full of hardened pros, and Jimmy would say to us, 'If you have the ball, wherever you are on the field, you are attacking. If you are a wing-half, you are a waiter in a restaurant; your job is to service the forwards.'

I took a lot from Jimmy when I became a manager and so did Malcolm Allison, who – although we would fall out badly – was one of my heroes. Jimmy preached close control, the ball passed constantly between two, on your toes, left foot, right foot, always ready to turn. He would have you turning, dragging the ball back, all the things that would become standard practice over time. If you see 'master coaches' at work now, the chances are that they will be overseeing an embellishment of what Jimmy Hogan once taught.

One thing I never became a fan of was the warm-up. When I managed Manchester United, the team was afflicted by a spate of hamstring injuries and I mentioned it to Ron Pickering, who was involved with British Athletics at the time. He said British athletes had the same problem and the suspicion was it was all the stretching they were doing before competing.

Now you see footballers warm up for twenty minutes before a match, and how many times do you hear there has been a late substitution because somebody has been 'injured in the warm-up'? I used to warm up in the dressing room and, while I can't imagine he modelled his career on mine, so did Andrea Pirlo. 'Masturbation for conditioning coaches,' he called the sight of an entire football team stretching before kick-off.

I had gone to Aston Villa from Wolves. I was doing some coaching at a local school with a mate of mine called Herbie Smith, who played for the Villa and asked me if I fancied moving. There was a bit of controversy but the Villa fixed me up with a job as an apprentice toolmaker at BSA. This enabled me to play in the Birmingham Works League, which was then the biggest football league in the world, with 24 divisions. I played for the county first team and they tried to persuade me to remain as an amateur because they were sure I would get an England Amateur cap.

I wasn't bothered about England Amateur caps. I wanted to play first-team professional football, a prospect that receded dramatically when Joe Mercer became manager of Aston Villa in December 1958.

He got rid of twenty of us. We learned about it from the back page of the *Birmingham Mail*. Every one of us who had been sacked had our photo in the paper. It looked like an appeal from Interpol, although at the time we felt like Aston Villa's least wanted.

# TWO

AFTER I LEFT ASTON VILLA I WAS GIVEN SEVERAL OFFERS BUT the one that interested me most came from Oxford.

It wasn't called Oxford but Headington United then, and they weren't even part of the Football League. I had never been anywhere like it. The football grounds I knew were tucked in behind rows of terraced houses but when I was trying to find the Manor Ground, what confused me was I was surrounded by trees and fields. I thought I might stick it out for six months. I stayed twelve years.

The main reason I went and the main reason I stayed was that Headington had an extraordinary manager called Arthur Turner.

Arthur was the most successful manager in Birmingham City's history. He had won them promotion and in the following season taken them to the 1956 FA Cup final against Manchester City, the one in which Bert Trautmann broke his neck. From there Birmingham had competed in the Fairs Cup, reached the semi-finals and were only knocked out by Barcelona in a replay after the tie ended up 4–4 on aggregate.

But Birmingham's chairman, Harry Morris, decided to make some changes at St Andrew's which saw Turner being made joint-manager. Arthur only discovered this through the press and, eventually, not long before I was shown the door by Villa, he resigned.

It might seem extraordinary that someone should voluntarily go from games against Barcelona to the Southern League, but the thing about non-league football was that it had no maximum wage.

Aston Villa's star player was Peter McParland and when I went to Headington I found myself on only three pounds a week less than him. When Leeds gave Turner a way back to the First Division by offering him the manager's job, the board at Headington were able to keep him by bettering the money. He was on £3,000 a year, a sizeable salary for the time, a little bit less than the cost of my home, which was a new-build bungalow in Wheatley. Leeds gave the job to Don Revie.

There was a lot of money in non-league football in the late 1950s and Bath City, who beat us to the Southern League title in my first season at Headington, had more than most.

In 1958, Stan Mortensen went to Bath for about £80 a week, whereas at Blackpool he would have been on about £20. Charlie Fleming, who was called 'Cannonball Charlie' for the power of his shooting, left Sunderland in his prime to go to Bath for three or four times the money he was making at Roker Park. They had Tony Book playing at right-back.

Oxford was a thriving, vibrant place, based around the Morris works at Cowley. I would describe the team as a kind of Wimbledon who could play a bit. Because the money was so good, the core of that team stayed together. Things were always happening at Oxford, whether it was a cup run or promotion challenge. We were elected to the Football League in 1962, reached the quarter-finals of the FA Cup two years later, and by 1968 we were in the Second Division.

I had chances to leave. In 1964 Tony Kay, the Everton captain, was imprisoned and banned for life following a betting scandal while he was at Sheffield Wednesday. Their manager, Harry Catterick, had identified me as Kay's replacement.

I was never told. I only found out because an Oxford director came to my house pleading with me not to go. I had no idea what he was talking about: 'Go where?' Manchester City and Newcastle both made offers that never made it past Oxford's board.

What Arthur was good at, and one thing I learned from him, was that he was very strong on getting players in with character. You never saw him from one game to the next. If you'd lost, you'd get a bollocking on Saturday night. If you'd won, you'd get a 'well done' and a little speech that would invariably contain the words: 'your success is my success'. Then he would clear off and you wouldn't see him again until the next match day.

He made me captain when I was twenty and, if things weren't going well, he would single four people out at half-time. It would be me, the goalie, the big left-back Pat Quartermain, or the centre-forward Bud Houghton, and he would go for us. Turner did it because he knew he would get a reaction; that we would go out wanting to show him he was wrong.

It was a technique I picked up on. When I was manager of Manchester United, we faced Watford at Old Trafford just before we were due to play in the 1983 FA Cup final and they were murdering us. Graham Taylor had shifted his centre-half, Richard Jobson, to play almost as a right-winger and just before the interval he missed an absolute open goal that should have given Watford the lead.

Their two midfielders were Les Taylor and Kenny Jackett; ours were Ray Wilkins and Bryan Robson. I said to Ray I wanted more pace: 'I want it quicker, you're fiddling with the ball, we have to hit the front quicker.' I kept it precise and technical.

Then I turned to Robbo. 'When are you going to start playing?'

'What do you mean?'

'I meant what I said. When are you bloody well going to start playing?'

'I am playing.'

'No, you're not. Les Taylor used to clean my boots at Oxford and, I'll tell you what, he wasn't much cop at that and now he's absolutely burying you.'

'I am not having you talk to me like that.'

'I don't care what you think. You either get it done in the next fifteen minutes or you're off.'

He was magnificent in the second half, we won and when it was all over I greeted him, arms outstretched, saying, 'That's the Bryan Robson we all love and adore.' He called me a bastard because then he knew why I'd gone for him in the dressing room.

You couldn't have talked to Ray Wilkins like that. He wouldn't know how to take it.

Even though I learned a lot from Arthur, management did not seem an immediate option. Six or seven years into my career at Oxford, I was offered a job at a big builders' merchants. I would do an hour or two's work in the morning just before I went into training. In the afternoons I'd be on the phone, make some house calls or spend some time in the office.

I learned a lot from that, more than you'd probably imagine. How to conduct yourself in meetings, for example – and I was quite good at selling. They put me on paints and sent me to a course right by West Ham's training ground at Chadwell Heath.

Then one day, I was told that if I wanted a job as sales manager, full time, I could have it. It seemed appealing because this was the first pre-season when I'd gone back without the usual zest for football. It was 1971 and we'd taken Oxford to a position where they were well established in the Second Division but we knew that was as far as we would go.

I was also doing some coaching, at the technical college and at Witney Town, where a mate paid me a fiver, and I ended up being practically full time in the evenings. When Bill Foulkes got the job a few years later, he found himself on £100 a week.

There were more lucrative football jobs in the offing. Reading and Crewe both offered me a player-manager's position. John Bond asked me to come to Bournemouth with him as a player-coach.

Then, I got a call from John Nash, a man who looked and talked like Alfred Hitchcock. He wanted me to manage Kettering Town in the Southern League Division One North. I wasn't interested. 'Come and talk to me,' he said. So I went to meet him in Bedford. He offered me £5,000 a year (about £70,000 in today's terms) and a car, and laid down some pretty ambitious plans for what he wanted done at Rockingham

Road. I would be the highest-paid manager in English football outside Division One.

I was mulling this over in the car, driving back home, and then suddenly pulled over to a red telephone box and rang my old man. 'If you don't have a go, you might never know,' said my dad.

So I found myself as a football manager and ended up signing the smallest contract, in terms of words, of my professional life. 'You will run the football team and be responsible for it.'

Nash had made his money in the Stock Exchange but, unusually, he didn't work in the City of London but in Kettering. He was up all hours, playing the Japanese markets. In 1976, under his chairmanship Kettering became the first club to have shirt sponsorship. We would turn up in Aquascutum blazers, the coach that we took to away games was top of the range, immaculately kitted out, and we would stop for a pre-match meal in some lovely restaurants. One lad at Dover came over to me and said, 'When we're playing you, we feel like we're playing the Arsenal.'

Kettering had a board of four. One was a surgeon, one was a broker, and one was the leader of the local Labour Party. Nash had stood as a Conservative candidate for Kettering in the 1955 general election and allowed me into the board meetings, which I found fascinating.

In one year, the club made £100,000 through a share issue, which even today would be an astonishing sum of money. The gates were big – around 4,000 – and the commercial department, who ran the lottery, brought in a lot of cash.

It allowed them to build the Main Stand that dominates the ground. The aim was get into the Football League and after successive promotions we had our chance. Now, we would have qualified automatically; then you had to be voted in and usually you were up against the team that had finished bottom of the Fourth Division. In 1973 we were up against Darlington and the following year, Workington Town.

We had been promised Nottingham Forest's vote but their representative's car broke down on the way to meeting so it was never cast. Workington survived until 1977 when they lost their place to Wimbledon.

Our big rivals for election were Yeovil. They were managed by Cec Irwin, who devised a stunt that when they came to Rockingham Road, the players should line up in front of the cameras each with a letter on his shirt. It spelled out: 'Elect Yeovil'. I got to hear of this and we gathered every football we could find in the ground, piled them up in the tunnel and, when Yeovil lined up for their photo-call, we shot them as hard and as straight at them as we could.

Arthur Turner had left Oxford by then but I employed him as a scout and to use his knowledge of the game. In 1972 we signed Roy Clayton from Oxford for £8,000 – which would be more than £100,000 today. Roy had just played against Manchester United in the League Cup and now here he was at Rockingham Road, where he became a catalyst for a lot of our success.

I'd also identified a kid at Northampton called Phil Neal. I agreed a fee of £6,000 for him. Northampton used to play on a Friday night and I went over to see their manager, Billy Baxter, because I wanted to play Phil against Weymouth on the Saturday.

He said Neal had to play the Friday game and in the days afterwards Northampton kept messing me about until I got a call from John Nash saying, 'Don't bother, we don't deal with people like that.' Whenever I see Phil, who signed for someone called Bob Paisley and became the most decorated footballer in Liverpool's history, I always remind him what he missed out on.

I was phoned up by John Nash, who asked me if I could buy a player from Chelmsford, Eddie Dilsworth, a big, black winger. We would pay £34,000 for him and Chelmsford would buy him back a year later for £30,000. When I went to Essex with Nash's cheque in my briefcase, it was all designed to reduce Kettering's profits so we paid less corporation tax. It was a problem few non-league clubs have to wrestle with today.

The problems Eddie brought to Kettering were not the sort any kind of manager should have to deal with. An hour and a half before kick-off, I got a call from him saying he couldn't play because he'd been arrested for fraud. He was acquitted, but he didn't make kick-off.

Whether it was exchanging a player for a lawnmower because, frankly, that was the best thing Stevenage had to sell, or wondering how one of your best players might escape the attentions of Essex Police, non-league football was an education, the kind that fewer and fewer top-flight managers are likely ever to experience.

One of the people I talk to most often about football is Garry Pendrey, who played for and managed Birmingham. He said to me, 'You wouldn't have got the Manchester United job now because you wouldn't have got the West Brom job. A Premier League club now would not dare to appoint someone from League One.'

And yet when I was at Old Trafford two of the great English clubs, Manchester United and Tottenham, were run by former non-league managers – me and David Pleat.

I was responsible for David's last game as a non-league manager with Nuneaton Borough. We beat them 4–0 and I was playing sweeper and, frankly, I could have played in a dicky bow.

After the match, one of our directors came up to me and said, 'Could you go and look after their manager. There has been a bit of a hoo-ha in their dressing room and I think the manager's been finished.'

I took David across to the bowling centre we had at Kettering and he started to go through the game with me, convinced Nuneaton had been unlucky to lose. I have a theory that, if you've lost 1–0, you might have an excuse. To explain away a 2–0 defeat, it would have to be something extraordinary. But he had lost by four. After he had explained at length about how Nuneaton could have drawn 4–4, I said, rather cruelly given the circumstances, 'David, if that's what you think, you're entitled to the sack.'

# THREE

FOR CHRISTMAS 1974 I GOT A FOOTBALL LEAGUE CLUB.
Cambridge United were not in the Football League by very much –
they were bottom of the Fourth Division – but they were in it. Perhaps
Kettering's successive failures to be elected had made me ready to move.

My brother Graham, who had played for me at Rockingham Road
and with me at Oxford, had been on loan to Cambridge and become
friendly with the club's vice-chairman, Reg Smart, who was the real
power in the club and would later become chairman at the Abbey
Stadium.

He rang to tell me that Bill Leivers had finished at Cambridge and
would I be interested in the job. I said I would actually and, although
they offered me the job there and then, I still had to apply for it in writing.

My first six months at Cambridge were unbelievable. Cambridge
had been bumping along the bottom when I arrived but they ultimately
missed out on promotion by three points. Of the final 24 matches we lost
two and yet some of our football was absolutely hopeless. I kept watching
this team, wondering, 'When are we going to pass to one another?'

There wasn't much skill but there was a lot of grit, tackling and hard
work – and given our limitations there had to be. When I first came to the
Abbey I was greeted by Nigel Cassidy, who I'd played with at Oxford and

who I'd been out with loads of times. 'It's great to have you here,' he said.

'It won't be great for you, Cass,' I said. 'You're great socially but I don't think you're a player.' I loved Nigel but he really wasn't my type of footballer, in the same way Tony Cascarino wasn't at Aston Villa. By way of compensation, I did manage to fix him up with a move to Colorado with Denver Dynamos.

There were one or two players who stood out. Brendon Batson, who had come to Cambridge from Arsenal, was there and so was Bobby Shinton, a centre-forward who would go on to play for Newcastle – but not before he was stopped by police on suspicion of being the Yorkshire Ripper. That was one of his easier problems to sort out and Shints had many.

When the 1975/76 season began, we were favourites to win the league, but I had my doubts because you couldn't sustain what Cambridge had done for a few months over a whole season. There was a decent pitch at the Abbey Stadium and I felt we needed some footballers who could pass.

Leicestershire won the County Championship in 1975 and I was at Grace Road a lot, not to watch the cricket but to try to sign Chris Balderstone, among the very last of a line who combined professional careers in our summer and winter games. He had just played in Carlisle's only season of top-flight football and I saw Chris as the type of player who could control a game. 'You're not here again,' his captain, Ray Illingworth, would say with a bit of exasperation.

I didn't get him because Balderstone went to Doncaster, but within a few weeks I had signed Steve Fallon, who had played as an amateur for me at Kettering but who was to become an outstanding centre-half at Cambridge. He was a plasterer by trade and would often turn up for games in his overalls.

He was on the bench for my last game at Kettering, an FA Cup replay that saw us beat Swansea 3–1, and my final words to him were: 'Don't you dare sign for anyone because I am coming right back for you.'

I bought two other teenagers, Steve Spriggs from Huddersfield and Alan Biley from Luton, all for £250 signing-on fees. They became the backbone of the Cambridge side that went through the leagues. Had I got Balderstone, I may not have signed any of them.

Reg Smart was the power behind the throne but the man who signed the cheques was the chairman, David Rushton, who would invariably be holding a cigarette whose ash was twice as long as the cigarette itself and which would, with relentless inevitability, topple into his suit.

Board meetings at Manchester United used to take half an hour. West Brom's were slightly longer and Kettering's, because of John Nash, had been brilliantly organised. Cambridge's would drone on forever. They would put on huge buffets, which were just as well because once we were there for eight hours.

Smart was an abrasive character and would have frequent arguments with Rushton. One of the directors, Paddy Harris, whom we called 'The Colonel' because of his military demeanour and who had been at the club since forever, suddenly picked up his cane and began walking around the boardroom table, smashing the tip of it between the people seated around it, shouting, 'You do not talk to my chairman like that.'

My hunch about not being able to sustain our form proved correct. We bottomed out and Cambridge finished thirteenth in 1976. However, the young players were starting to come good and we signed Dave Stringer from Norwich to bolster the defence, Tommy Finney from Sunderland in midfield and a former Arsenal goalkeeper, Malcolm Webster, who had been recommended by Brendon Batson.

We hit the ground running and by Christmas we were clear and on the way to becoming the leading goal scorers in the Football League. But I felt we needed a centre-forward to get us over the line and Paddy Crerand, who was managing Northampton at the time, had a striker called Jim Hall that he didn't fancy. Hall had become the leading scorer in Peterborough's history but he was past thirty and Paddy was quite happy to loan him to us.

He was a big, gangly, left-footed lad and when he arrived at Cambridge, he came over to me and said, 'I can't run, I can't tackle and I don't work. All I do is score goals.' I told him those weren't bad attributes for a centre-forward and he scored me 15 in 24 games.

It probably wouldn't be allowed now, but my assistant John Docherty and I used to run a book with the players. We used to shout out in the dressing room, 'Who wants to back themselves for a clean sheet?' or 'Who wants to back themselves for a goal?' and John and I would give out some odds. We never, incidentally, called out if anyone fancied backing themselves to lose.

Jim Hall always used to back a clean sheet and if we were at Southend or somewhere like that and they had a corner, he would race back to defend it if we hadn't conceded. By February, we knew we were going up and then it became a matter of winning the Fourth Division title. I remember those final months as a long party.

Jim had to go back to Northampton when his loan was up in the summer of 1977 and I didn't think he was quite up to the Third Division. I went to Brighton for his replacement. Sammy Morgan was a big Irish scrapper of a centre-forward who had helped Brighton win promotion from the Third Division. I was convinced that if we signed him, he would do the same for Cambridge.

It was the biggest transfer gamble I ever took. Morgan cost £15,000 and Cambridge's total cash assets at the time were £2,000. I told the board that if they signed him, we would get out of the Third Division as well and we did – finishing runners-up behind Wrexham, although by then I had moved to West Brom and John Docherty was in charge.

Despite our upward trajectory, money was still tight at the Abbey. Coincidentally, we drew Brighton in the League Cup. We drew the first game and we drew the second and Alan Mullery, who was managing Brighton, and I had to toss to decide where the replay would be staged. I told him to forget the toss. We would play at the Goldstone Ground, because if Cambridge played at home we might only get 6,000 but 20,000 would watch at Brighton and then the gate money was split. We used the money to pay for Sammy Morgan.

Sammy was a teacher from Belfast who had been to the same school as George Best. He wore contact lenses and in the dressing room at Colchester we were agonising about how to tell him he was dropped.

Sammy was still fiddling with his contact lenses when John Docherty went over to him and said, 'Don't bother, you won't be needing them.'

On one away trip there a card school going on at the back of the bus. Sammy walked down the back of the coach, tipped the card table over and, with the money and cards everywhere, shouted, 'Come on, let's have a yarn.'

One of my big mates at the time was the chairman of Bradford City, Bob Martin. When we won promotion to the Third Division in 1977, Bradford sneaked up in fourth. I used to rib him that Cambridge would take them up on our coat-tails and we'd beat teams on Bradford's behalf.

Our first game of the new season saw us away at Valley Parade. We were hammered. We lost 4–0 and when I went into the boardroom I saw Bob and I could tell he was trying to hold it back but, deep down, he was smug. 'Before you start,' I said to him, 'we will win this league and you will get relegated.'

Bob bit on that. 'You big-headed bastard, we have just stuffed you by four,' he grinned. As it turned out we finished second and Bradford went down.

I wasn't at the Abbey Stadium when Cambridge went into the Second Division. John Docherty, the Doc as we called him, steered them over the line. At the age of 38, I was a top-flight football manager, in charge of West Bromwich Albion.

My last game at Cambridge had been against Bradford in January 1978 and we thrashed them 4–1. Gary Newbon, who was to become head of sport at Central Television and was already a good friend, acted as a broker in the deal.

Before beating Bradford, our previous game, funnily enough, had been at Oxford on the Wednesday night and the following day I was due to meet the West Brom delegation, the chairman Bert Millichip and the vice-chairman Tom Silk, in the Randolph Hotel.

We'd won at the Manor Ground and I'd gone out with a few of my old mates; waking up on Thursday morning it dawned on me I had no suit for the interview. I phoned a friend of mine who owned a clothes shop and said, 'You'd better get me a suit.' It fitted and so did the job, although we agreed to keep it quiet until the weekend.

I still had to go to the Hawthorns for a formal interview for a job I and everyone else at West Brom already knew I had. When I arrived at the ground I was met by Sid Lucas, one of the old directors, who looked at me conspiratorially and said, 'Come and see what we've got for you.' He led the way to a blue Jaguar, a 3.4. 'Rather better than what you're driving at the moment,' he added with a grin.

'Not really, Sid. I've got one of those but it's a 4.2.'

It is a strange thing to say but as a manager you want to inherit a struggling team. If a club is heading for relegation, the directors are starting to panic and, realistically, they see you as the only hope of avoiding it. They will give you carte blanche to do what you want, they will back your decisions and, if they've got the money, they'll back you in the transfer market.

West Bromwich Albion were the only club that when I took over were doing OK. In this scenario, you have to question yourself more. Decisions are harder to push through because you get the response: 'But this is the way we've always done it, Ron.'

The foundations had been laid by John Giles, who had won West Brom promotion and established them in the First Division. The man I replaced was Ronnie Allen, who as a player had captained them to the FA Cup and second place in the league behind Wolves in 1954. But he had left the Hawthorns to accept a job managing the Saudi Arabian national side, which opened the door for me.

The one to the dressing room led into a poky space and the Smethwick End was open terracing but it was a club heading upwards. The changes I made at first were relatively minor. Under John Giles, West Brom had developed a slow, patient build-up to their play, but they had a couple of fast forwards coming through in Laurie Cunningham and Cyrille Regis, and I wanted the ball played quickly to their feet.

The only signing I made was Brendon Batson. At the time, West Brom's right-back was a lad called Paddy Mulligan and, although I'd never thought of Brendon as a top-flight footballer, when I looked at Mulligan I thought to myself, 'Brendon can do all of this and he's miles quicker.'

When I made my move to Cambridge for him, I made sure I did it on a Thursday. Reg Smart, the vice-chairman, was the power at the Abbey Stadium and I knew what he did on a Thursday. It would be golf and then out on the razzle. He most certainly would not be in his office.

I rang the chairman, David Rushton, who was definitely the weaker of the two. I offered him £25,000 for Batson. Rushton hummed and harred until I said, 'It's £28,000 but it has to be done today.'

He agreed and I phoned Brendon, who was having a do at his house. When I offered him West Brom, he thought I was having him on but I said, 'No, I'm not, but I want you at the Hawthorns to have your medical today.' Brendon got himself across to Birmingham immediately and the deal was done.

The next day I got a ferocious phone call from Reg Smart. Amid all the invective the phrase: 'You know he's worth ten times that, you bastard,' kept being repeated. Had Reg not taken himself off to Newmarket golf course, we would still probably have done a deal but the figure would have been nearer £150,000. It was an expensive round.

When I became manager of West Bromwich Albion, I came into Brian Clough's orbit. He regarded himself as leader of the Midlands pack and, if you were a Midlands manager, he'd be interested in you.

He could be a bugger to deal with. I once called him about a transfer and he said, 'Have you talked to the player?'

'No, Brian, I'm trying to do this properly. I'll talk to his club first and then I'll put it to him.'

'Do it properly then. First you tap the player and then you talk to me.'

I loved Cloughie, loved his company and then I became manager of Manchester United and, apart from business, he didn't exchange a civil word with me. You'd offer him your hand after a game and he'd walk away.

Then two weeks after I'd left United, I was asked to do a game at Nottingham Forest for television. I bumped into him in the corridors afterwards and I heard that nasal twang: 'Hey, get in my office, we'll have a drink together. There's lots I want to talk to you about.' This was the man who for five years would not have given me the time of day.

If you were manager of one of the Big Four at the time – Manchester United, Liverpool, Tottenham or Arsenal – then Cloughie didn't want to know you. It might have been because he was jealous of their budget but, more than that, it was because he wanted a siege mentality at the City Ground. He wanted a very clear line between 'Them' and 'Us'.

There might have been something extra about me being manager of Manchester United because he felt, maybe with some justification, that he should have had the job when Sir Matt Busby left.

I enjoyed our talks and throughout my career I was never afraid to ask for advice. At Cambridge I would meet up with Bill Nicholson after a game and buttonhole him in a corridor. Bill had stepped down as Spurs manager by that time but he was still connected with the club in a scouting capacity. Nicholson had this reputation as a dour, hard man but if you got him on the game and you talked to him over a cup of tea, he could be brilliant.

When I was at Cambridge, I would call Bill Shankly at home every Thursday afternoon. I'd tell John Docherty to pick up the other phone in the office and murmur, 'Don't say a word, just listen.' He was no longer Liverpool manager, football was the only thing in his life and he loved the game. He would talk to you for an hour.

It was sad in a way because he had quit on an impulse and regretted it. Liverpool should have offered him something but John Smith, the chairman, might have seen him as a threat. When I took over at West Brom, I would bring him down to the Hawthorns to watch games and speak to the lads in the dressing room. When we went down to Highbury to play Ipswich in the FA Cup semi-final in 1978, I invited Shankly on to the team bus and to sit with the players at the pre-match meal. I just wanted them to listen to him talking football.

We lost that semi-final 3–1, and I felt a bit stitched up. Not by Ipswich but by the BBC. I was called up by *Football Focus* who told me that they would be interviewing all four managers left in the FA Cup on the steps leading up to the Royal Box at Wembley and talking to them about how it would feel to lift the trophy. I was told Bobby Robson would be going up the steps with his whole team.

I thought the publicity couldn't do West Brom any harm but it did. When the programme came out, I was the only one they had interviewed. We were about to play a semi-final and here I was talking about how it would feel when West Brom got our hands on the trophy. It looked appalling. I don't think they even asked any of the other three managers.

The semi-final was not noticeably much better. We'd recently played Ipswich at Portman Road, they'd been leading 2–0 quite comfortably but conceded twice in the last eight minutes, and that led to Bobby Robson storming off in a cold fury.

They had gone to Highbury wanting to prove a point and they did. Within eight minutes they were a goal up and our captain, John Wile, had split his head open in a collision with Brian Talbot; the blood was streaming down his face and into his shirt. Eventually, he had to come off.

At 2–1 down we had a chance to take it to a replay. We'd worked on an elaborate free-kick routine in training and it worked, giving Willie Johnston an unmissable chance that he promptly missed. John Wark scored in the last minute and that was that.

Kevin Beattie was one of the reasons Ipswich won the FA Cup in 1978. He had been out virtually all season with a cartilage injury but he came back and had a tremendous game in the semi-final and played beautifully against Arsenal at Wembley.

Then, they would deal with cartilages in the old way, by opening up the knee. You were then told to give the player six to seven weeks to recover. I used to give them eight or nine. Ipswich said they brought Beattie back in three weeks. It might have won them the FA Cup but they were the kinds of decisions that contributed to the wrecking of what should have been a tremendous career.

# FOUR

WE FINISHED THE SEASON WITH A TOUR OF CHINA. I WAS quite keen not to go but it was tied up with an Anglo-Chinese export drive. England, who had failed to qualify for the World Cup in Argentina, were due to tour China but it fell through and Bert Millichip volunteered West Brom. It was a big political coup for him because we were the first team from the Western world to go there since the Chinese Revolution but it turned into the longest, hardest three weeks of my life under the slogan of: 'Friendship First, Football Second'.

It was two years after Chairman Mao's death and China was still a nation of bicycles and boiler suits. The BBC filmed a documentary on the tour for *The World About Us* programme. It produced the classic quote from John Trewick – 'When you've seen one wall, you've seen them all' – when we were taken to the Great Wall, which was always held up as example of how thick footballers are. But John said it as a joke.

The matches were played in absolute silence and if anyone in the crowd made a noise there would be an announcement on the Tannoy telling them to be quiet. We played in Canton, in Peking in front of 80,000, and Shanghai, and at half-time they would bring in ice creams to the dressing room because it was so hot.

China was then completely different. Carlton Palmer lives in Shanghai now and tells me it is one of the biggest, most frantic cities in the world. Now it takes hours to cross the city by car. Then you went by bike.

The *Daily Mail* sent its chief sportswriter, Ian Wooldridge, on the tour. He had no real interest in the football, he just wanted to see the way of life in China. After he had filed his report, Wooldridge received an official complaint from the Chinese authorities, taking him to task for what he had written about the People's Republic. They thought it slanderous.

The trouble was the piece hadn't actually appeared in the *Daily Mail* yet. Ian had phoned over his copy from his hotel room on the Saturday for Monday's paper. It was Sunday when the Chinese lodged their complaint. They had been bugging his telephone.

There was a guy seconded to us from the Chinese secret service and when we were taken up the Yangtze for a tour, he would stand on deck taking notes on every ship that passed us. James Bond he wasn't.

In 1978, one in every five was a member of the Communist Party and we also had a party functionary attached to the team, who had no time for the Western way of life. I thought I could get him our side, plying him with cigars. Every day he became less and less hard-line and when we had to leave he was virtually crying his eyes out. I had the feeling he wanted to leave with us.

The most Westernised person we encountered was the coach of the Chinese national side, who had worked in Yugoslavia. You could sense he had to be careful in what he said but he did want to talk at length to us.

China is now aa popular destination for the Premier League's leading clubs as they chase their money. In the summer of 2016 both Manchester City and Manchester United would play out there but the Far East, with its heat, humidity and flight after flight on chartered jets, has never struck me as ideal preparation for an English winter.

I used to like quick four- or five-day trips to places like Holland, where you would play a Dutch team, a German team and maybe one from South America in one of the Amsterdam tournaments. Then you'd go back to your own training camp. I still think that's the best way – there is far too much importance put on pre-season results.

In the summer of 1985 the Heysel ban meant Manchester United couldn't do a pre-season abroad, we lost virtually all our warm-up games – our best display was in a draw at Hereford – and we were beaten comfortably by Everton in the Charity Shield. We began the season by winning our first ten matches.

Willie Johnston didn't go to China. His destination was Argentina and the World Cup and he came back rather quicker than he'd hoped. He had taken Reactivan, which was a hay fever cure and had the reputation of a pick-me-up, although I doubt Willie would have known. I imagine one of the Scotland players would have passed them to him and said, 'Take them, Willie, they're fine.' They weren't fine and Willie was sent home in disgrace after Scotland had lost their opening game to Peru.

The day he was due to arrive at Heathrow was Colin Addison's first day as my assistant and we had to go to London to pick Willie up. Bob Wilson had asked if he could interview Willie for the BBC and he was in our car as we drove towards Heathrow.

Because I'd seen it in the movies, I'd asked permission to drive up to the aircraft on the tarmac and pick Willie up when he stepped down from the plane, but that was very firmly refused.

The world's press was at the airport and you couldn't move for journalists. They managed to get me on to the pier so I would be the first person Willie would see when he got off the plane.

I saw him, grabbed him and told him every reporter on earth was around the corner. 'Just keep a straight face and keep on walking.'

He had two big cases with him and I grabbed them and, as we turned the corner to face a wall of reporters, I began swinging them to try and clear a path through them so we could make our escape. I managed to bowl over Ray Maloney, a reporter for *News at Ten*, before we got to the car.

Then, in the rear-view mirror of the Jaguar, I saw two motorcyclists who, as we drove towards Shepherd's Bush, kept pace with us. When we slowed, they slowed. When I turned down a one-way street so did they. Eventually, when we pulled into Broadcasting House, they were right behind us. They were outriders sent by the BBC to make sure we made the interview.

The whole circus had a big impact on Willie Johnston. He never played for Scotland again, and he was banned from European football just as West Brom had qualified for the UEFA Cup. The whole thing dragged him down and eventually we decided to move him on and Willie ended up at Vancouver Whitecaps, playing in the North American Soccer League.

In 1978, the flights that really excited me were not to China or North America but to Europe. West Bromwich Albion had finished sixth in the First Division and qualified for the UEFA Cup. It was then a fantastic competition. Only one club, the champions, qualified for the European Cup and, if you were lucky, you might not play anyone serious. But you got up to four from the major leagues going into the UEFA Cup. You couldn't miss them.

We joined a party that included AC Milan, Ajax, Arsenal and Benfica. It was won by Borussia Mönchengladbach, who had faced Liverpool in the European Cup final the year before.

I wanted every European trip to be an event. Before every flight I would offer the players a glass of champagne at Birmingham airport – although Tony Brown, who hated flying, would have considerably more than one. I wanted the players to look forward to the European games, not regard them as a chore they had to get through.

Our first flight took us to Istanbul, and a stop-off at the Intercontinental Hotel. We were due to play Galatasaray but, because of crowd trouble, UEFA had forced them to shift the game to Izmir. I was in the foyer of the Intercontinental with Sid Lucas, one of our directors who was a right old Brummie, and he said to me in that thick accent, 'I don't think the hotel in Izmir will be up to this kind of standard.'

He was right. One of the journalists, Ray Matts from the *Daily Mail*, came downstairs to complain there was a bat in his room. The hotel had no dining room so for our pre-match meal I took the lads across the road to a street café. Izmir may not have had much in the way of hotel accommodation but it did possess a lido and I suggested to the lads that they had a swimming competition – anything to avoid spending time in our Turkish Fawlty Towers. When we finally reached the stadium, we beat Galatasaray 3–1.

After seeing off Braga, we faced Valencia in November. They were a fabulous side with Rainer Bonhof and Mario Kempes and for the first twenty minutes in the Mestalla they battered us. Dario Felman scored for Valencia, but somehow we managed to stay on our feet and gradually we dragged ourselves back into the match. By the time it was half an hour old, Laurie Cunningham was ripping them apart.

This was the night that Laurie sold himself to Real Madrid. They would have looked at him, they would have watched him and been mesmerised by what they saw. We drew 1–1 and it was December by the time of the return at the Hawthorns.

It was the start of what was to be one of the longest, hardest winters this country had known and as I watched Valencia train with their players in gloves and mufflers I was pretty confident West Brom would be going through. We beat them 2–0. Tony Brown scored twice, one an early penalty, the other from a cross supplied by Laurie.

West Bromwich Albion were on fire but outside it was getting colder and colder. We should have won the league that year and we would have won it but for the winter, which had turned into a long, deep freeze. Politically, it became known as the Winter of Discontent. In football, it did for West Brom's chances of becoming champions.

The way we were playing in December 1978 West Brom would have beaten any team in Europe. In that month we won five matches and had the other two, against Everton and Southampton, postponed because of snow. The games everyone remembers now are the ones at Highbury and Old Trafford. That match at Old Trafford is probably West Brom's most celebrated game since they won the FA Cup in 1968 and at the end even the Manchester United fans gave the team a standing ovation.

When I went to manage United 18 months later, that game was the first thing people wanted to talk about. It is a contest so ingrained in

West Brom's DNA that last year they staged a dinner to celebrate that one match.

It was the strangest game. We played beautiful, dominant football and yet United managed to score three times in the first half. To this day I don't quite know how.

Right on the stroke of half time, 3-2 down, we knocked a long ball down the middle, Len Cantello flicked it on. At that moment I thought I heard the half-time whistle and spun round to go back to the dressing room. When I looked up I saw Tony Brown take the ball round the keeper, Gary Bailey, and put it in the net. I just assumed it had been disallowed.

Once we were in the dressing room I told them, "You only have to keep playing like that and you'll equalise and, once you've done that, you'll win the game.'

Tony Brown looked at me quizzically and said, 'But gaffer, I have just equalised.'

'Well it won't be that hard to equalise then,' I said. I honestly thought there had been a whistle blown.

Tony Brown was a fanatical Manchester United fan and he scored twice that day. When the team bus pulled up at Old Trafford, he got out wearing a red shirt. I turned to him and said, 'are you playing for us or supporting them?'

Some of the football we played in that match was untouchable. Gary Bailey was United's man of the match and some of the saves he made, especially from Cyrille Regis, were astonishing. Without him, we might have scored anything between eight and ten.

What we had and what defenders all over the world hate is pace. Cyrille was as quick as anyone who has ever played the game and Laurie wasn't far behind. Bryan Robson used to say to me, 'We need to hold the ball up to give the midfield a chance to join the attack.'

I replied, 'You had better get up the pitch, then Robbo, because they ain't waiting.'

We had more than just pace. Derek Statham and Len Cantello were superb, underrated footballers. Cantello was Bryan Robson's hero, a man he adored playing alongside. People used to tell me that Tony Godden in goal was a bit of a weak link but he played more than 250 games on the bounce under several different managers so, if he had a weakness, he kept it pretty well disguised. We beat Arsenal 2–1 and Manchester United 5–3.

But for me the game I will always remember when I look back on that season was on New Year's Day against Bristol City. the Hawthorns was frozen and covered in snow – you wouldn't even consider playing today.

A couple of weeks before, I'd gone to the Adidas factory with a number of other managers. We flew into Strasbourg and crossed the border into Germany in a big old Mercedes as the snow came down, looking like something out of *The Ipcress File*.

They showed us these boots with moulded soles and dimpled, rubber studs and I took a pair away with me. They felt really good and when we were training I went over to Cyrille Regis, who was about my size, and said, 'Hey, big man, try on a pair of these.' Cyrille loved the boots.

The Adidas rep in England was a former West Brom goalkeeper, Graham Smith, who had played for me at Cambridge. I asked if he could get me a full set. They arrived just before we were due to play Bristol City at the Hawthorns. I was out on the pitch with Tony Collins, who was my assistant, later to become my chief scout at Manchester United, Alan Dicks, the Bristol City manager, and the referee.

Dicks and the referee thought the conditions ridiculous. As we were discussing it, Tony Brown came flying past shouting, 'Boss, we can't call this off.' I said to the referee, 'That man has played 750 games of football, he doesn't need another one.' It was half past two by then and a crowd was building up and so was the pressure on the referee to allow the match to start.

The corridor leading to the referee's room at the Hawthorns was made up of concrete slabs and, as I went to give him the team sheet, I heard this massed clattering coming from the away dressing room. Bristol City were coming out, wearing old, full-length studs.

Joe Royle had just signed for Bristol City. I'd met him on holiday and knew him quite well and he yelled, 'You can't play on this, Ron.'

'I don't what you're worried about,' I said. 'If you are frightened of getting hurt, all you have to do is stand still.'

The first time Joe did any running was in the 75th minute when Alan Dicks called him off. Len Cantello and Bryan Robson, using little give and goes, were almost unplayable. We beat them 3–1.

We then went to Norwich, drew 1–1 at Carrow Road and found ourselves top of the league. We didn't play in the league again for three weeks.

I was desperate to find any kind of match for us to play in. When I was a player at Oxford, I did a bit of coaching at Witney Town and they were giving a testimonial to one of their players, Trevor Stokes. I called them up and said, 'Tell you what, we'll play you.' I then heard that Nottingham Forest were desperate for a practice match so I called up Witney and asked if they minded West Bromwich Albion (who were then top of the league) playing the league champions on their pitch in a game that would be Trevor Francis's full debut after he had become the first £1m player in British football.

Witney's ground held a maximum of 2,000 but when West Brom and Forest pitched up for the testimonial, there must have been 7,000 milling around. It finished goalless but sticks in my mind as the most competitive friendly I have ever witnessed.

When I was managing Cambridge, I'd taken them away to Guernsey for a mid-season break and I got a call from the island to tell me that their pitches were OK. I mentioned it to Jim Smith, who was then managing Birmingham, and asked if he fancied coming over with us. We chartered a plane and put both teams on it – something which the insurers would definitely not allow now – and flew to the Channel Islands.

The sports paper in Birmingham, the *Argus*, decided they would put up the money for a trophy, which they called the Arctic Cup, in tribute to the Big Freeze. The hospitality in Guernsey was so lavish that the journalists who came with us – because there was little else to cover – said it was one of the best trips they had ever been on. The match ended with the organisers trying to persuade Jim and me to finish the match with a penalty shoot-out. I was game but Jim had I'm afraid sampled a little bit too much of the hospitality. The claret had done for him.

Our first game back was at Liverpool, who had been playing all through this. We were dreadfully rusty, still in three competitions and this was the first of eleven games we had to play in 30 days, including being knocked out of the UEFA Cup in the quarter-finals by Red Star Belgrade. It all caught up with us and we began to fall away.

Liverpool won the league with a record number of points in the days when you got two for a win. We lost our last two matches to finish third behind Nottingham Forest, who beat us 1–0 at the Hawthorns to secure the runners-up spot. West Brom were third with 59 points, which would have been enough to win the whole thing a couple of years before. But 1978/79 was our year and our season and we should have finished it as champions. We deserved something more than the Arctic Cup.

# FIVE

BRYAN ROBSON AND LAURIE CUNNINGHAM, THE TWO MEN
most associated with my time at West Bromwich Albion, were not in the
team when I arrived at the Hawthorns. We played the FA Cup semi-final
against Ipswich without either of them and without Len Cantello, who
was also to become an integral part of my team at the Albion.

West Brom had been doing pretty well when I arrived and I didn't
feel I could make too many changes. But after we lost our chance of
Wembley, I decided to be more radical. Brendon Batson came into the
side and the four of them formed the core of the team that started the
memorable 1978/79 season.

Robbo was good, he was 21 then but, if you'd asked me at the time, I
didn't think he would become the great midfielder he turned into at Old
Trafford. When he was in the reserves, I got a lot of offers for him; Ron
Saunders tried to take him to Aston Villa. But I always said no. The first
game he played for me was at centre-half, against Manchester United,
and I asked him to take care of Joe Jordan, which he did terrifically.
Once he got into his stride, you could see the promise and the potential.

England were slow to see what he was capable of. He was 23 when
he won his first cap and didn't go to the European Championships in
1980 and we didn't qualify for the tournament in 1984. But for that

and for injury, he would easily have surpassed the 90 caps he did win. The FA's inability to recognise Robbo's capabilities became such that the *Birmingham Mail* ran a campaign for Ron Greenwood to give him an international call-up.

Just before he signed for Manchester United, I saw him score his first international goal, in a World Cup qualifier in Norway. It got lost in the wash, partly because England were beaten and partly because of a rant by the Norwegian commentator, Bjorge Lillelien, which contained the immortal line: 'Maggie Thatcher, your boys took one hell of a beating.' It sticks in my mind even more because I was sitting next to Mr Lillelein when he launched into his tirade.

A big influence in Robson's career was Arnold Muhren. Robbo had been brought up always to play to feet whereas Muhren taught him the value of playing into space.

Arnold was one of the most underrated footballers Manchester United have ever had. I'd long wanted to sign him and had gone out to Holland to watch Frans Thijssen, whom Bobby Robson brought to Ipswich with Muhren in 1979. Thijssen was playing for Twente Enschede at the time but the trouble with scouting Dutch football was that if you watched games away from Amsterdam and Rotterdam, they seemed to be playing on park pitches.

You'd be astonished by the small size of the ground, you'd wonder what the standard was and then you'd see someone who played in the 1978 World Cup final.

I missed out on Thijssen then but I kept tabs on Muhren and after Bobby Robson left Ipswich, the club allowed both of them to leave. He was not a typical Dutch footballer. There was no hint of arrogance about him, he didn't want to give you his opinion about the game; Arnold was very quiet and very professional.

Sometimes at Manchester United, I would play Arnold and Robbo together, sometimes I'd have Bryan going through the middle between the strikers, Norman Whiteside and Frank Stapleton, which is a tactic I devised after we'd been knocked out of the FA Cup at Bournemouth.

Robbo was easy to coach. He was a man's man. The trick was to get him up for a game by challenging him. You could goad him, you could provoke him, he would respond and often he would respond magnificently. As he grew older, he became more ready to speak out in the dressing room and took more of an interest in the kids coming through, who would address him as 'Mr Robson'.

He, in turn, was very respectful of authority. He had a very close relationship with his dad, whom he leaned on a lot for advice. His father was a long-distance lorry driver from County Durham and by rights he should have been on the *Herald of Free Enterprise* when it sank off Zeebrugge. He arrived in the port, he was tired and thought he'd have a few drinks and take a later ferry. When he was a boy, Bryan used to go out with his father in the cab and his brother Gary, who was my last signing as manager of West Brom.

Bryan was a better manager than he has been given credit for. He took Middlesbrough to three Wembley finals in the space of twelve months and had their chief executive not completely misread the situation, Middlesbrough would not have failed to turn up for a match at Blackburn, they would not have been docked three points and they would not have been relegated.

He was undermined as manager when Terry Venables was brought in as the club's first-team coach and although Robbo was still technically the club's manager he had lost all authority. In the early summer of 2001, Steve McClaren was all set up to succeed Harry Redknapp as manager of West Ham until he got a call from Fergie telling him not to take the job because Middlesbrough wanted him. I was in Milan for the Champions League final between Bayern Munich and Valencia and overheard Fergie giving McClaren the advice over the phone.

At the time Robbo was out in Hong Kong with his chairman, Steve Gibson, playing in a five-a-side tournament. I rang a mutual friend and told him, 'Get hold of Robbo because he's got a problem.' The word came back that Bryan thought he was fine. He'd had a word with Steve Gibson and he was still manager of Middlesbrough. Soon afterwards, he found he wasn't. What hurt him was that Gibson had not had the courage to front it up. A man like Bryan Robson deserved better.

Robbo and Laurie only really had one season together, 1978/79, the one which should have seen us win the championship. West Brom were one of the first clubs to be hit by freedom of contract. In 1979 Len Cantello moved to Bolton while Laurie Cunningham was transferred to another, rather more famous, club that played in all white.

The president of Real Madrid, Luis de Carlos, accompanied by the club's general manager, came to the Black Country to see me and Bert Millichip about Laurie. We decided to hold the negotiations in my house, where they offered £250,000 for him. I had a Yorkshire terrier and when they mentioned the fee, he started growling at the Madrid delegation and I said to them, '*Senores*, not even the dog likes your offer.'

I had a phone in the kitchen and they asked if they could use it. I went with them while they called back to Madrid and there, by the phone, was a brown envelope. I grabbed a pen and wrote £1.5 million on the back of it. They crossed it out and wrote £450,000. The haggling went on but when they mentioned £950,000 I said yes, provided we could have two friendlies with Real Madrid – an option that the Albion, in their wisdom, never took up.

Laurie was a lovely lad. He and the rest of what we called the Three Degrees – Brendon Batson and Cyrille Regis – became the target of racist chanting from the terraces. I used to ask some of the other lads whether they had heard any racism on the pitch but their answer was usually no.

The racism was worst at Leeds but, from my experience of Elland Road, they didn't like anyone. Cyrille silenced them with two fabulous goals and, to give the crowd their due, they applauded him and us off the pitch.

Before we played Everton we would always get a letter, obviously written by someone very erudite, urging me not to select any 'gorillas' when we came to Goodison Park. Often, before we played Everton, Cyrille would come over and say, 'Has our mate written yet, gaffer?' and I would show him the letter.

Sometimes they would have bananas thrown at them. Cyrille picked one up and ate it. At West Ham, Brendon stuffed one down his shorts. Humour to me is the best way to disarm a racist because one thing I do know is that racists don't always have the sharpest intellect. They dish out hate and they expect hate back. They don't know how to respond to humour.

Leeds and West Ham were one thing but a lot of other grounds loved watching us play and we became a lot of people's second team. We could always get a result at Arsenal or Tottenham, and White Hart Lane appreciated the style.

Laurie had style. Everyone had him down as an extrovert but it masked a shyness. When he started at Leyton Orient, he was never a great timekeeper and he would be regularly fined. Laurie would go down the local discos and get the money back dancing. When he was at West Brom, he was a great dresser. Once, before we played Middlesbrough, he and Cyrille turned up in lovely suits over a polo-neck sweater. I told them that, stylish as they were, I'd prefer ties, and for the next game they wore ties. There was never a time when Laurie caused me disciplinary problems.

The difference between Laurie and Cyrille was that Cyrille had been an electrician, he had seen the real world. If the pressures of football and the racism bothered him, he didn't let it show. He would make jokes about dusting off his toolbox and his monkey wrench. 'I can always go back,' he would say.

Laurie was more of a loner and I spent a lot of time with him because he would usually stay behind to do extra training. I would sit and talk with him; he had a very deep interest in football and football tactics.

He shone at Madrid until he was seriously injured and then I don't think Real Madrid looked after him particularly well. When Gareth Bale moved to Madrid, he would have had a player liaison officer to sort out everything for him away from the club. Laurie had none of that. He was left to his own devices.

Though he was never much of a drinker, Laurie would take himself off to nightclubs and, even in a city as big as Madrid, it would get back to the management. I last saw him in the spring of 1989. He had joined Rayo Vallecano on the south side of Madrid and helped them to promotion. I was in the city to commentate on a game at the Bernabeu and we went out for dinner. 'When I go back to the Bernabeu, I am going to show them what they missed,' he said. He was hard, determined and within a few weeks he was dead in a car crash.

It wasn't the first one he had been involved with. Cyrille told me he had been in an accident with Laurie a few weeks before his Seat Ibiza came off the road on the A6 northwest of Madrid.

Once he dropped out of the first team at Real Madrid, they offered me Laurie back on loan. I was at Manchester United then, preparing for the 1983 FA Cup final, Stevie Coppell's career had been prematurely cut short by injury and Laurie seemed a decent bet at Old Trafford. He should have played at Wembley against Brighton.

He'd played a few games for United before and we were preparing for the final on the Bank of England pitches at Roehampton. Laurie had done twenty sprints and then turned to me and said he didn't think he was fit enough to play. What might have come into his mind was that we only had one substitute. 'I don't want to risk it,' he said. 'I'll let the boys down if my hamstring goes.'

There was a phrase I'd always use as a yardstick if a player came up to me and said he was injured. 'Would you play in the cup final?' I was offering Laurie a place in the cup final. Had he been selfish, a typical forward out for glory, he would have taken it.

I wanted him to play. He moved so beautifully. I used to say of him that he could run on snow and not leave a mark. Although he had lost some of his pace, Laurie would still have glided across a surface like Wembley's. The choice of replacements was Ashley Grimes, Alan Davies and, funnily enough, Paul McGrath, who had scored twice in midfield against Luton in a game that he otherwise performed hopelessly in.

Laurie had such an advantage on a big pitch. I had watched him play for Ron Greenwood's England against Wales in May 1979; he was stopping and rolling the ball inside the full-back for Ray Wilkins to run on to. 'What on earth are you playing like that for?'

'That's what the manager wants me to do.'

'You should just get the ball and run at the full-back. That's why you're in the team. That's your strength, running, dribbling. Get at them!'

'But they don't want me to.'

There is one memory of Laurie that will stick with me forever. After we beat Valencia in December 1978, we played Wolves in the Black Country derby and won 3–0. I invited the players and their wives back to my home for a pre-Christmas party.

The house had a swimming pool and at two in the morning Laurie, Cyrille and Tony Godden ran over and jumped into it. When I went over to the pool next morning, it had frozen over. When I think of Laurie Cunningham it is of him running towards the pool with Cyrille and Tony and leaping and laughing into the water.

Without Laurie, West Brom lacked something and there were other losses. Cyrille and Derek Statham began the 1979/80 season with knee injuries, we brought in Peter Barnes and Gary Owen from Manchester City and John Deehan from Aston Villa. But with the injuries and without Laurie, West Brom had suddenly become a team in transition and by Christmas 1979 we were bottom of the league.

I bought in Remi Moses and in January we faced Crystal Palace at Selhurst Park and were two down with five minutes to go. To this day, I believe that had we lost that match, West Brom would have been relegated because the bottom would have fallen out of the club. In those last five minutes, Ally Robertson and Big Cyrille scored and we drew.

Those remaining four months were I think the best I have ever managed. From January onwards we lost two league games, against Aston Villa, who could always get something at the Hawthorns, and on the last day of the season at home to Stoke.

There was panic in the boardroom but I kept telling the dressing room to keep playing and remember the style of football that had brought them such success the season before. Barnes and Owen couldn't believe the mess they had walked into but I kept saying, 'It will come, you're good enough.'

We finished tenth and the following season, the year that Aston Villa became champions, West Brom ended up fourth. I rounded off the season with a trip to Paris to watch Laurie and Real Madrid lose to Liverpool in the European Cup final. It was the night I learned I was to become manager of Manchester United.

# SIX

JOE MELLING WAS AN OLD-SCHOOL FOOTBALL REPORTER with bags of contacts and he was intent on tracking me down. I was with West Brom in Florida on an end-of-season tour and he tried my hotel.

'I am afraid Mr Atkinson is not in his room.'

'Could you try the poolside bar?'

I was passed the phone and a sandpaper-rough voice told me that Lawrie McMenemy had turned down the job of Manchester United manager. 'But he was nailed on. Last time I heard he was looking at houses in Wilmslow.'

'Not any more. Have you been sounded out?'

I hadn't, though I did tell Joe that the day before I'd gone to watch Tampa Bay play Fort Lauderdale and Frank Worthington had come up to me and said, 'I know who the next Manchester United manager is.'

'Who is it?'

'It's you.'

That's all I could tell Joe but on our return from Florida I'd gone straight to Paris to see Liverpool win the European Cup at the Parc des Princes. That night I had a phone call from another journalist, John Maddock, telling me that Martin Edwards wanted to meet me. I took a flight to Manchester and met Martin at John's house. He offered me the job.

Martin Edwards was the best chairman I ever worked with. He was very supportive to me, as he later was to Alex Ferguson. My brother told me once that, if you check the records, my first four years at Old Trafford were the most successful of any manager of Manchester United. The top four meant nothing in 1981 but, if you judge a club by today's standards, United would never have been out of the Champions League positions.

Since winning the European Cup in 1968, Manchester United had finished in the top four twice – in 1976 and 1980. The only significant piece of silverware they'd won in those thirteen years had been the FA Cup, when they beat Liverpool in 1977. There had been two others finals, both lost.

Edwards told me the priority was to bring regular European football back to Old Trafford. In May 1969, Manchester United had beaten AC Milan 1–0 in the semi-final of the European Cup at Old Trafford in front of 63,000 – a result that wasn't enough to overturn the defeat they'd suffered at the San Siro. For the great European teams that Sir Matt Busby had fashioned over the years that was it. Since then, Manchester United had featured in three European campaigns, none of which made it past the second round.

What might have made Edwards keen to pursue me was that in my three-and-a-half years at the Hawthorns West Brom had qualified for Europe three times. In our first meeting, Martin said to me, 'We have got to become a European side again.'

I didn't feel I was stepping into something special or that I had a lot to live up to. When news of the appointment got out, one journalist said to me, 'You're leaving a better team.' West Brom made no real attempt to keep me. The directors were lovely people but naive – we used to call them the Lavender Hill Mob after the Ealing comedy.

They'd let not just *my* contract run down but that of virtually the entire team. Towards the end of my time at the Hawthorns, I had gone to try to negotiate a longer contract for Bryan Robson and one or two of the others only to be told: 'I think he's here for long enough, don't you?'

The year I became manager of Manchester United, 1981, was the high-water mark for English managers. Bob Paisley had just won his third European Cup with Liverpool. Ron Saunders had won the championship with Aston Villa, Bobby Robson had lifted the UEFA Cup with Ipswich. Howard Kendall had been appointed at Everton. Keith Burkinshaw had just won the FA Cup with Tottenham. Lawrie McMenemy was at Southampton while Brian Clough, the man I regarded as the best of the lot, ruled Nottingham Forest.

It had developed into an astonishingly competitive league. From 1977 to the year of the Heysel disaster in 1985, the European Cup was won by an English team in every season bar one. There had never before and never would be again such a period of dominance by English clubs. When people look back on the years between Busby and Fergie, they talk about Manchester United's quest for the Holy Grail of the league title. By 1981, the league title wasn't an issue at Old Trafford – Manchester United just wanted to compete.

When Jose Mourinho was touting himself for the Manchester United job, the objection against him was that he has little interest in youth development, but these days, when you live and die in the here and now, I have some sympathy for him.

Even when I was at Villa Park, they were a club who set great store by their academy and youth development whenever their lack of spending was questioned. I used to say to the board, 'I can't tell the fans that we'll have a great team in six years because they will tell me that in that case they will come and watch the team in six years' time. We have to have a team on the park now – and then we can look at the youth team.'

That was pretty much my attitude at Manchester United and from what I understand about how Mourinho operates we were quite similar. The emphasis was getting the first team right, keeping the sessions bright and bubbly with a lot of ball work and just a few physical sessions. We brought through a few very good young players in Mark Hughes, Norman Whiteside and Clayton Blackmore but the absolute priority in 1981 was the first team.

Dave Sexton had been sacked after Manchester United had won

their last seven matches, which seems astonishing until you realise that in April 1981, United finished eighth. If West Brom had won their last seven matches of the season, we would have won the championship.

The legend has grown up that Sexton was sacked because the football Manchester United played was so excruciatingly dull, a charge I always thought unfair. He was a brilliant coach, the best I have ever worked with, and had he not been my predecessor at United, I would have tried to take him with me to Old Trafford. When I was manager of Aston Villa, I brought him on to my coaching staff and asked him to work twice a week with every player under 21 years of age.

People used to watch Dwight Yorke in his prime and say what a natural footballer he was. He wasn't that much of a natural – he played as Dave Sexton taught him to play, and Dave did a lot of work with Steve Froggatt and Graham Fenton, a forward who should have become a much better player than he did.

I would come across just to watch his training sessions in the same way that I used to watch Jo Venglos's sessions when he was in charge of Czechoslovakia during the 1980 European Championship – which I found fascinating and a lot more organised than England's. Mostly the sessions I watched reinforced the way I coached, but Dave had the ability to come up with different things. I always liked my strikers split up with one on the shoulder of the second centre-half, whereas Brian Clough liked his strikers together.

Dave used to work on the ploy that if the ball came into the leading man, rather than go outside, as most defenders would expect, he should go inside. A defender would always go with you if you turned outwards but if you went inside they might not and then the second striker could make a diagonal run to a straight pass.

He had a reputation as a quiet man who would read poetry but we used to have a Christmas party for the youth players at Aston Villa and before the dinner we'd have a game on one of the Astroturf pitches. I'd bring in a few of the backroom staff like Peter Withe or Andy Gray and invite Terry Cooper from Birmingham and Phil Neal from Coventry and we'd play against the kids. After the dinner there'd be various turns and Dave would get up and begin singing old Cockney songs.

The problem he had at Manchester United was that for him training was a deeply serious business and the players he had would not want to spend an hour and a half doing repetitive drills. Young players were different, and that's why he had such success as a youth-team coach.

My problems at Manchester United were mainly to do with the age of the players. The big names at Old Trafford were all coming to the end of their careers. Martin Buchan and Lou Macari were 32; Joe Jordan had been sold to AC Milan and, while Gordon McQueen was only 29, he was increasingly prone to injury.

I annoyed the shareholders immediately by saying that what this club required was major surgery. United had spent significant sums of money but they'd done so in a haphazard way. I brought in Bryan Robson and Remi Moses from West Brom, John Gidman from Everton and Frank Stapleton from Arsenal. The total cost was around £3m. Martin said he would stand the bill if we recouped much of the money by Christmas.

Jimmy Nicholl left for Sunderland and, in February 1982, Stoke paid £350,000 for Sammy McIlroy. Sammy had felt threatened by Robbo's arrival but I'd envisaged a different role for him on the left of a bank of four forwards. I'd long been an admirer of John Robertson at Nottingham Forest and I thought there was a role for an experienced, intelligent midfielder on the left and that Sammy could do for us what Robertson had done for Clough. He wouldn't be a flying winger, he'd just have to use his brain.

On the day in October when we brought a table and chairs out on to the pitch at Old Trafford to sign Bryan, Sammy scored a hat-trick, which shows you what he thought of the deal. We were playing Wolves and the £1.5m fee United had paid West Brom broke by £31,000 the English record transfer fee Wolves had paid for Andy Gray.

Just before we went out on to the pitch for the photocall, Jack Taylor, the 1974 World Cup final referee who was now the commercial director at Molineux, handed me a gold pen. It was the one Wolves had used to sign Andy and he suggested we use to it to close the deal for Robbo.

It was the deal that persuaded Sir Matt Busby to resign from the board at Manchester United. He didn't flounce out, it wasn't a vindictive move, he still came to the games and he would still pop in for a cup of tea. However, he could not believe any player was worth £1.5m. 'I can't come to terms with what's happening in the game,' he said. To Sir Matt, money was poisoning football.

I told the board that Bryan Robson was not a gamble. They were wary because the October before they had spent £1.25m on Garry Birtles, who had scored precisely no goals in his first season at Manchester United. Garry did OK for me in his second season but they felt burned by the experience.

I didn't keep any of Dave Sexton's backroom staff, mainly because when I was at West Brom I'd heard them badmouth their own manager, which I thought scandalous. I took Mick Brown and Brian Whitehouse with me from West Brom to be my assistants.

The choice of your backroom staff depended on where you were. At Cambridge, I had John Docherty, a very bright, inventive coach who had worked under Dave Sexton at Queens Park Rangers. At West Brom, the idea was to keep everything bubbly and fun. If you brought a tactics board into a team meeting, they thought you would be playing bingo. Colin Addison, who was a real livewire, was a perfect number two.

Richie Barker, who I later brought in from Luton to be my number two at Sheffield Wednesday, was completely different to me. Chalk and cheese. Off the field he could be great fun, but he was very serious about training. Richie would complain that when he had set up a session for some intricate three-quarters work in the last third of the pitch, I would come out and say, 'It's a lovely day, let's have a bit of zip and push. Let's have a blast on the banjo.'

I didn't like a big backroom staff. After training we'd have a meeting with the assistant, the youth-team coach and the physio to talk things through. I was quite prepared for people to argue their case but once the decision was made, that would be the party line.

Norman Whiteside had come to Old Trafford the same day as I did. He didn't play a lot of reserve-team football, though he did play alongside Mark Hughes in the FA Youth Cup. He was sixteen but he looked twenty-five, single-minded and very mature for his years.

In April 1982, towards the end of my first season at Old Trafford, we were due to play at Brighton. I told the staff I was thinking of putting Whiteside in the first team a few days before his seventeenth birthday. Brian, who always wanted to push young players through, wasn't enthusiastic. Mick Brown was undecided.

I cut through the attempt at democracy by shouting, 'I don't give a toss what any of you think; he's in.' I made Norman a substitute at the Goldstone Ground, where he came on for the final twelve minutes to become the third-youngest player in Manchester United's history. He started the final home game of the season, scoring in a 2–0 win over Stoke, and a month later he was in Spain with the Northern Ireland side to overtake Pele as the World Cup's youngest footballer.

Sometimes, the backroom discussions would make me change my mind. We had bought Peter Beardsley from Vancouver Whitecaps. He had played in one League Cup game, against Bournemouth, before going back to Canada. In 1983 we had the opportunity to bring him back to Old Trafford for £500,000. Again we had a meeting about it and Brian Whitehouse pointed out that if we brought Beardsley in he would block the progress of another young player – Mark Hughes. To me this seemed a point very well made.

Peter was then 22 and he had given us no real indication of the footballer he was to become. He went to Newcastle, who were then in the Second Division, but he was protected by footballers of the calibre of Kevin Keegan, Chris Waddle and Terry McDermott and allowed to find his feet. He might not have had that at Manchester United.

Maybe I should have kept Syd Owen, who had discovered Hughes, as my youth-team coach but instead I brought in Eric Harrison, who became the man who nurtured the boys who were to make the modern Manchester United – Ryan Giggs, Nicky Butt, Paul Scholes, David

Beckham and the Neville brothers. The Class of '92. Beckham kept in touch with Eric years after he left Manchester United. Bryan Robson notwithstanding, Eric was probably the best signing I ever made for the club.

Eric had been first-team coach at Everton and possessed a fearsome temper that saw him sent to the stands on more than one occasion. I had known Eric since our days in National Service. Growing up just after the war, kids had various war heroes from Field Marshal Montgomery to Squadron Leader Douglas Bader. Mine was Sergeant Bilko.

I spent less than four months of my two years' service at the camp in Abingdon and the rest of it playing football. I would train with Oxford United in the morning and then go into the camp, where I worked as a telephonist.

One week I played thirteen matches. There was an Inter-Command Week where you played twice a day. I was picked to play for the RAF against the Army at Molineux. The Army had Ron Yeats, Jim Baxter, Alex Young – Everton's 'Golden Vision' – and Chris Crowe, who would play as an inside-forward for Leeds and Wolves. Our biggest star was Derek Stokes, who played for Huddersfield and Bradford. We beat them by four.

Mostly, the RAF teams were made up of lower-league players like Tommy Burlison, who turned out for Hartlepool. I remember going up to the Northeast and asking if anyone had heard of him. 'You mean Lord Burlison?' came the reply. He became treasurer of the Labour Party.

The success didn't last for the RAF. We had to play an FA XI at Peterborough and lost 13–0. Ted Farmer, who but for injury would have been one of Wolverhampton Wanderers' great strikers, scored four. Bobby Tambling, one of Chelsea's finest forwards, hit six. I was captain and had a right go at Barry Jackson, a centre-half who was to become a stalwart at York City.

'Get it sorted, Barry,' I kept yelling at him.

'I can't take any risks, Ron,' he said. 'I'm being demobbed today. I'm out.'

Although Eric Harrison's great successes were to come after I'd left United, we got to two FA Youth Cup finals and did bring two top-class young players through in Mark Hughes and Norman Whiteside. There should have been a third in Nicky Wood but he was forced to retire at 22 with a back injury. Arnold Muhren thought he would become the next Trevor Francis.

Eric was a disciplinarian who encouraged people to play. We had a very promising centre-half called Simon Ratcliffe who went away to Lilleshall, where the FA's director of coaching, Charles Hughes, insisted the ball always be played long. When Simon came back to train with us at the Cliff, Eric couldn't believe what he was trying to do. 'You should be playing to feet, not belting it up the pitch.'

Simon, a very intelligent lad who was to have a good career at Brentford, explained that this was precisely what he had been told to do when he was with the England youth set-up. Eric and I decided to call the FA and tell them that if this was what they were teaching, not to bother picking Manchester United players.

The FA were wedded to the long ball, which they claimed brought players into what they called POMO (Position of Maximum Opportunity), and Charles Hughes's response when his tactics were challenged was: 'Imagine if the Brazilians ever get hold of this; they'd be unstoppable.'

Fergie used to say that of all his players the one he could never see becoming a manager was Mark Hughes. When I ran Manchester United, I didn't even think Sparky would make a player. On Thursday afternoons we would get the kids in the gym for a five-a-side.

It was how I got to know them and, as soon as I saw Norman, I knew what he would become. In Sparky, I saw a sullen, morose young man. We played Sunderland in an FA Youth Cup tie. I was watching alongside Sir Matt Busby and Jim McGregor, the club physio, and I was being driven up the wall by Hughes's sheer inertia. If there is one thing I cannot stand in a footballer it is lack of enthusiasm. Lack of ability, I can accept. He was of no use to me.

'He'll be OK,' was Sir Matt's verdict, while McGregor was even more fulsome in his opinion about Hughes's potential. Sunderland had a defender called Neil Aspin, who was good enough to play more than 200 games for Leeds. In the last minute, goalless, Sparky accelerates away from him, goes past six players and squares the ball for Norman, who taps it in.

I turned to Sir Matt and Jim and said, 'I think my judgement might have been a bit premature.'

# SEVEN

IT WAS THE JOB YOU DREAMED OF, MANAGER OF MANCHES-
ter United. The start, however, was not the stuff of dreams.

My predecessor, Dave Sexton, had been fired after winning his last
seven games. I managed to win none of my first four. We finally beat
Swansea in mid-September, which marked Garry Birtles' first goal for
the club nearly a year after he joined Manchester United. Then the
team began to find its rhythm, we won five of the next six and finished
third, behind Liverpool and Ipswich.

I had arrived at Old Trafford slap in the middle of Liverpool's long
dominance of the English game. The rise of Everton as their strongest
challengers meant that from 1976 to 1989 – thirteen long years – the
league championship only twice left Merseyside.

Some argue that the team that won the Double in 1986 was Liverpool's strongest but for me the side that Joe Fagan coached to the
league title, the League Cup and the European Cup two years before
was supreme. The central defensive partnership of Alan Hansen and
Mark Lawrenson was as good as I have ever seen, with Phil Neal and
Alan Kennedy at full-back. Graeme Souness dominated the midfield
with Kenny Dalglish and Ian Rush pushing through.

Liverpool then had no real weaknesses you could work on and they could play either way. They could pass the ball beautifully or they could fight with you. In one-off games we could usually hold our own. In the ten league games Manchester United played Liverpool in my years at Old Trafford, we lost only once. We knocked them out of the FA Cup in 1985 and they beat us in the League Cup final two years before.

My pre-match team talk to Ray Wilkins or Arnold Muhren would be the same and, if it was delivered in the dressing room at Anfield, I would emphasise it: 'I don't want you coming in at half-time complaining Souness has kicked you because I can tell you now he is going to kick you. But what I can also promise you is that they – and here I would point to Bryan Robson and Remi Moses – will kick him back.'

Naturally, Robbo dominated any field he walked upon but Liverpool had a great respect for little Remi. Off the pitch, Remi was as quiet as a mouse, on it he would go toe-to-toe with anybody. If you showed any kind of fear or hesitation, Liverpool would smell it.

The key to that Liverpool side was Phil Neal. People used to say Liverpool did not possess a playmaker but, if you watched them carefully, Phil set up a lot of their moves, often because he had nobody directly up against him.

The first time we played Liverpool, at Anfield in October 1981, I put Stevie Coppell on the left wing and told him to run at Neal and give him no time on the ball. Neal didn't hurt us and we won that match 2–1. Once Arnold arrived, I had a naturally left-sided midfielder to employ against Neal.

Their manager, Bob Paisley, was a hard man to fathom. Every phrase he uttered seemed to contain the word 'doings' and there was seldom much he said that struck you as memorable but he won everything, including three European Cups in four years. I find it extraordinary that Manchester United saw Matt Busby, Bobby Charlton and Alex Ferguson knighted but Shankly and Paisley were plain 'Bill' and 'Bob'. They deserved as much recognition.

Paisley signed for Liverpool in 1939, so he had been at the club for 35 years before he took over as manager. He knew Anfield and Melwood intimately, which was instrumental to his success. In the transfer market he had a great eye for a footballer and as a former physio he could spot physical weaknesses early on. His teams rarely seemed to lose players to injury.

Liverpool then were an insular club, difficult to get to know, but while there was considerable animosity between the two sets of fans and even the two cities, the two sets of players got on brilliantly. Bryan and Terry McDermott were especially close and I would go up to Robbo and say within McDermott's earshot that Terry was a bad influence and he should stay clear of any social activities that were being planned.

Under me, Manchester United were a team that were supposed to have drunk themselves into oblivion, usually at the Four Seasons Hotel by the airport. That was a massive exaggeration. When he was at West Brom, Robbo would be involved in out-of-hours activities with some of the team but early on in his time at United he came to me and said, 'Gaffer, I can't get any of them to go out.' I told him to keep trying.

Alcohol was part of the temper of the times in English football and it was not confined to Manchester United. I once joined Liverpool on a post-season tour to Israel and I could not believe the amounts of booze that team put away, even those you wouldn't suspect were big drinkers, like Hansen. Everton won two championships with Howard Kendall taking his team to Chinatown most Tuesday afternoons.

What those teams had was great spirit, they had tempo and they had mental strength. It was one of the qualities that enabled English teams to dominate the European Cup before Heysel brought it all to a horrible end.

I was showing a young kid a documentary MUTV made on Norman Whiteside called *Fearless* which featured a game against Arsenal in which the two teams kicked lumps out of each other. I said, 'I bet you can't believe we used to play like this?'

Those kinds of games gave you the mental strength to be hit, get back on your feet and carry on as if nothing had happened. I see a lot of those qualities in the way Leicester made their extraordinary challenge for the Premier League title. They had a high tempo, they passed direct and they had a bit of flair in the way they went about their business. If you put the Wimbledon of 1988 into today's Premier League, how many would cope with them?

The foundations of Leicester's success under Claudio Ranieri was laid down by Nigel Pearson when he kept them in the Premier League in 2015. They play long balls, they pass quickly into space, but one thing they don't do is pass the ball square. Robert Huth and Wes Morgan do not, as so many modern centre-halves do, pass to each other.

As a manager, if we were in trouble I used to tell my team to let our opponents' centre-halves have the ball, seal off the midfield and see what they did with it. Usually, they would do very little. The most common pass made by Arsenal is from Per Mertesacker to Laurent Koscielny, across the face of their own area. At Manchester United, Chris Smalling's first instinct is to pass to Daley Blind.

I have never once seen Mertesacker take the ball on the outside of his right foot, aiming for a midfielder who would then try to find the leading man. It was the kind of move Bobby Moore made his speciality. It wasn't a long-ball tactic but it cut opponents out of the game by fizzing the ball up the field. Argentina won the World Cup in 1978 with precisely this kind of football.

I love passing football as much as I despised Charles Hughes's long-ball dogma at the FA but some clubs have made it a fetish, forgetting that the kind of passing that matters is progressive passing. Too often, it becomes a cul-de-sac, a road Manchester United increasingly travelled down under Louis van Gaal.

In August 2015, United began the season at home to Tottenham. If I had been Mauricio Pochettino, my team talk would have centred around the opening twenty minutes. 'Manchester United have a point to prove, they are at home and they are going to come at you. The first twenty minutes will be about staying in the match.'

Instead of which, Manchester United spent the opening twenty minutes essentially passing the ball among themselves, usually square and with no threat to the opposition. Tottenham would have wondered what they had to fear and, although Manchester United won that game, through a Kyle Walker own-goal, it set the pattern for a season in which Manchester United's play at Old Trafford became increasingly ponderous.

In 1983 Bob Paisley won his last trophies as manager of Liverpool, his sixth league championship and his third League Cup. Although we did not lose a single game at Old Trafford, there was not much we could have done to stop Liverpool winning the league – Manchester United finished third, twelve points behind. But we should have won the League Cup.

It was my first Wembley final, we were playing Liverpool; we took the lead through Norman Whiteside and held it until fifteen minutes from time. By the end United were essentially down to nine players with Gordon McQueen employed as a makeshift centre-forward. Just before the end of normal time, Gordon found himself clear on goal only to be cleaned out by Bruce Grobbelaar in an assault that had shades of Harald Schumacher and Patrick Battiston in the previous summer's World Cup. The difference was that Gordon was not carried off on a stretcher and Grobbelaar was at least booked. Ronnie Whelan won Liverpool the cup with a beautiful, curling shot into the top corner and Paisley led his team up to collect the trophy.

It was a season when Manchester United faltered at the last. We had lost the League Cup in extra time and if we had got a point in the last game of the season, we would have finished second, which would have been a fair achievement – something United had done only once since 1968. We were 2–1 up at Meadow Lane and Notts County scored twice in the last couple of minutes to rob us of the runners-up spot.

Then there was the FA Cup final against Brighton, which is remembered for a piece of commentary: 'Smith must score'. It was 2–2 and late in extra time and when Gordon Smith made to shoot I turned to the bench and shouted, 'Great, we've got fuck all from the season.' When I looked up the shot had been saved; we won the replay 4–0. Bryan

Robson was unplayable. Manchester United had their first trophy in six years and I had the first of my managerial career.

The defence of that trophy lasted one match, a third-round tie at Bournemouth, which Harry Redknapp has never allowed anyone to forget. United were in the middle of a very tight schedule which meant that if we drew we would have had to play Bournemouth on the Tuesday and then Queens Park Rangers in a televised league game on the Friday.

As we approached the hour mark on a horrible pitch at Dean Court it was goalless and Jim McGregor turned to me on the bench and said, 'We could really do without the replay.' Bournemouth then scored twice in a couple of minutes and I said to Jim, 'I'll take that replay now.'

The defeat by Bournemouth overshadowed the fact that we had just been knocked out of the League Cup by Oxford in a second replay.

The ups and downs of a football season can be summarised by the fact that we failed to beat Oxford and Bournemouth but we did overcome Barcelona. It was the quarter-finals of the Cup Winners' Cup and we had lost the first leg 2–0 at the Nou Camp.

The evening of 21 March 1984 has gone down as one of the great nights in Manchester United's history. Judging from those who said they were there, there must have been 200,000 at Old Trafford, rather than the 58,000 who paid, but Martin Edwards came over to me on the morning of the match and said, 'You will hear a noise tonight the likes of which you have never experienced before.'

The sound of Old Trafford was incredible. It was quite high-pitched and shrill. It drowned out everything and coloured everyone's impressions of the night. If you watch Manchester United versus Barcelona with the sound turned down, it is quite an ordinary match. However, the noise and the emotion of the night made it something extraordinary.

I don't think we actually played that well except for the fact that we knew Barcelona had a weakness at corners and it was something we exploited. We worked on near-post flicks in training and our first goal came from that – a corner from Ray Wilkins, flicked on by Graeme Hogg and buried by Robbo.

We scored twice more in the second half but if Barcelona had scored, they would have gone through on the away-goals rule. I'd put Mark Hughes on with eighteen minutes remaining and the first thing Sparky did was to foul Barcelona's winger, Lobo Carrasco, in the box. It was a penalty and the referee played on. And then virtually with the last kick of the game, Bernd Schuster drove in a shot that Gary Bailey went the length of the goal to try to save and it clipped the edge of the post and went wide.

Then, on the final whistle, a wave of people came on to the pitch; Robbo was carried off shoulder-high. Peter Reid, who was then at his peak with Everton, had come to the game and found himself standing on his seat shouting his head off. Emotion was spilling everywhere and behind the scenes it was bedlam.

There were four teams left in the Cup Winners' Cup – Aberdeen, Juventus, Manchester United and Porto. We drew not just Juventus but probably the best Juve team there has ever been. Claudio Gentile, Gaetano Scirea and Antonio Cabrini were the men around whom the defence rested. Their midfield consisted of players of the quality of Marco Tardelli, Massimo Bonini and Michel Platini, who supplied a front two of Paolo Rossi and Zbigniew Boniek. Five of their players had won the World Cup for Italy two years before.

Manchester United, by contrast, were crumbling. Wilkins was suspended for the home leg and Arnold Muhren was injured, which left a great weight on Bryan Robson's shoulders. I was in my office at the Cliff, doing an interview with some Italian journalists, when I glanced out of the window to see the team coming back from training.

Robbo turned and whacked a ball to where the ball bag was and, in doing so, tore his hamstring. Of the midfield I would have liked to have picked for the semi-final, only Remi Moses was available. I had to use my instincts to construct some kind of midfield to face what was possibly the best club side in the world.

John Gidman had just recovered from injury so I put him on the right, where he lasted twenty minutes before breaking down. Alongside him was Paul McGrath and Arthur Graham, who I had bought from Leeds when they were relegated. We drew 1–1 at Old Trafford and we were drawing 1–1 at the Stadio Communale until the final minute when Paolo Rossi pounced on a deflection and knocked us out.

The injuries didn't just cost Manchester United a chance of a European trophy, they cost us the league. When we beat Barcelona, United were then a point clear of Liverpool at the top. Liverpool, chasing the league and the European Cup, stumbled to the finish line, winning just four of their final ten games. Manchester United didn't stumble, we collapsed completely. Liverpool won four, we won two of the last ten to finish fourth behind Southampton and Nottingham Forest.

It was perhaps not the best piece of planning to send an exhausted, injured team around the world for an end-of-season trip to Australia but that's where we went. We played a game in Hong Kong and then Robbo, Mike Duxbury and Ray Wilkins went back to play for England against Scotland in the Home Internationals while the rest of a very depleted party carried on to Sydney.

When we touched down at Sydney airport, I did a television interview where the first question was: 'Mr Atkinson, I'd like to welcome you and Manchester United to the World Series of Soccer.'

'The what?' I had about nine players with me and I wasn't well acquainted with half of them. I'd assumed we would be playing a few matches against some local sides. I said to the lads, 'When you get off the coach, keep walking around the bus just to make it look like there's a load of you.'

I spent the rest of the day on the phone trying to get players to come and guest for Manchester United while they were in Australia. I got hold of Frank Worthington, Peter Barnes and Tommy Hutchison – 'Ron's Flying Circus', as Gordon McQueen called it.

I took the first training session with Mick Brown and the lad driving the coach joining the players, while up in the stands we spotted the Australia manager, Frank Arok, spying on us. What he hoped to learn about Manchester United from that, God only knows.

We drew 0–0 against Australia at Sydney and by the time we faced the other teams who had been invited to the World Series, the reinforcements had come back from England duty. We beat Nottingham Forest in Melbourne and then went up to Surfers Paradise to stay in these beautiful apartments on the shores of the Pacific Ocean. One of our young players, Mark Dempsey, came over to me with a look of disbelief, saying, 'Gaffer, last year I was on holiday in Rhyl.'

We finished up playing Juventus, who had just won the Cup Winners' Cup, in Sydney and we were called to a press conference to promote the game. I told Gary Bailey and Gordon to put their tracksuits on and we'd go to the hotel to face the press.

Hitherto we'd been lucky to attract half a dozen journalists but this was like a film premiere. The auditorium was packed and when I went out on to the stage all I could see was this row of black-and-white tracksuits. The compere asked me and Giovanni Trapattoni to introduce our teams.

I pointed to Gary Bailey and Gordon McQueen, who had barely played in the last twelve months, and added, 'And of course we will be bringing some of the best young players England have produced – Stephen Pears, Mark Dempsey and Alan Davies.'

Trapattoni responded, 'We have Gentile, we have Tardelli, we have Cabrini, we have Boniek,' and he went on. The end of the season had seen constant speculation over Bryan Robson's future and Juventus had long wanted to take him to Turin. My first question was about Robbo.

'I can tell you there is absolutely no chance of Bryan Robson leaving Manchester United,' I said, and behind me Gentile, who was quite a character, began jumping up and down and hugging Boniek saying, 'Zibby, Zibby, your job is safe!'

We all went out in Sydney the night before the game, where we were joined by Joe Bugner and Dennis Lillee. Tardelli kept coming over and saying, 'Tomorrow night, no war, no war.' And none of us wanted a battle. The game was one of the dullest sporting events the

SCG can ever have staged until Peter Barnes in his wisdom decided to nutmeg first Tardelli and then Gentile. For the final five minutes it was Vietnam.

# EIGHT

AT THE HEART OF THE MANCHESTER UNITED SIDE I CREATED
were two men whom my successor, Alex Ferguson, found difficult to manage. I would disagree with Fergie; Norman Whiteside and Paul McGrath
were very easy to manage – when they were fit.

Paul suffered deeply from a traumatic childhood of foster homes and
appalling poverty in Dublin, the kind that never leaves you. It is impossible
to read his autobiography and not be moved by what he endured.

Norman was from Belfast and he had a very different upbringing, solid,
Protestant. By the age of sixteen he was astonishingly mature. But by the
time Norman was 26 he was behaving like a teenager. Their backgrounds
may have been very different but Paul and Norman got along very well.

Norman arrived almost on the day I was appointed at Old Trafford.
Unusually for the time, he played very little reserve-team football. He
almost went straight from the youth team to the first team and, but for
his injuries, Norman would have been one of the Old Trafford greats. He
was 25 when he finished, but packed an enormous amount into that time.
He played in two World Cups for Northern Ireland and won the FA Cup
twice with Manchester United. He would get whacked by defenders and
I would tell him to ignore it, to keep on playing, because Norman could
play like few others. Had he possessed a yard of pace, he might have the

best Manchester United player there has ever been.

Like a lot of good players who lack pace, Norman compensated with awareness. If you stopped the play, he could tell you where every player on the pitch was. His speed was in his head. Sometimes you see a quick player stop and look up before darting on. Norman would be prowling, always aware, always looking.

I will always remember watching Norman when Northern Ireland were playing Spain in Valencia during the 1982 World Cup. Norman had just turned seventeen and was facing Juanito, a winger from Real Madrid who was to be killed in a car crash at the age of 37. Norman tackled him so hard that Juanito almost finished up in King Juan Carlos's lap a few yards away.

The problem Norman and Paul suffered from was alcohol and that only became an issue when they were injured or away from the game and all the social invitations kept coming.

The first time I saw Norman take a drink, he had been playing for Manchester United for three years. After we had won the FA Cup in 1985, United went on a tour of the Caribbean, which began in Trinidad. We set up camp around the hotel pool and everybody was lolling around drinking Carib beer. I wasn't bothered, we would be playing a local team in Port of Spain, it had been a long, long season and we had just won back the FA Cup.

Then Mick Brown came over to me and said, 'Are you sure we are not playing Southampton? I've just bumped into Lew Chatterley (who was Lawrie McMenemy's number two) and they are training pretty hard.'

I said I would check with Majid Mohammed, an agent from Leeds who had organised the tour, and he confirmed Mick's worst suspicions – we ended up playing the Saints. I took Norman off after an hour and when he asked why, I told him it was to stop him looking a bigger prat than he was already. It was the first time I had seen Norman affected in any way by alcohol.

We went on to Jamaica and John Barnes had told us to look up his father, who was a colonel in the Jamaican army and had been involved in co-ordinating the Caribbean participation in the invasion of Grenada. Colonel Barnes said he would arrange for paratroopers to drop into the stadium with the match ball before kick-off. I have seen enough of these to know that if a paratrooper doesn't land in the centre circle, it is considered a fail. None of Colonel Barnes's men landed in the stadium. They disappeared behind the stands, taking the match ball with them.

McGrath was much older than Whiteside when he came to Manchester United – twenty-one as opposed to sixteen. There was never any doubt with Norman, the first time I saw him I just knew he would make it. But when I first saw Paul, I could see he had one or two decent attributes but I didn't know whether they would amount to anything.

At that time Ruud Gullit was starting to make a name for himself at Feyenoord and I thought that if Paul didn't make it as a centre-half, he might do a job where Gullit was playing, on the right-hand side of midfield. He scored twice against Luton just before the 1983 FA Cup final but otherwise played so badly I had to put him back to centre-half, although Jack Charlton sometimes played Paul in midfield for the Republic of Ireland.

Paul had pace and he had power. He became, for what my opinion is worth, the best centre-half the Premier League has seen. He had this great trick when the ball came across of back-heeling it in the air with his right foot. It was because his right knee was so knackered he could barely stand on it to kick with his left.

After I'd left Old Trafford, Manchester United tried to finish him. Fergie wanted him to cash in on the insurance, accept that his knee injury was chronic and in return for that Paul would get a pay-off and a testimonial in Dublin. Had they offered him a bit more money, I think Paul might have accepted, which would have meant his career would have been over in 1989, a few years before it reached its peak at Aston Villa.

I was at Sheffield Wednesday when I got wind that Paul's time at Old Trafford was coming to an end. I had just sold Ian Cranson to Stoke for £400,000, the kind of deal that makes you think you can swim the Channel, which meant I had some money. I phoned Alex and told him I would be interested in Paul for £100,000, which could go up depending on how he did at Hillsborough.

Fergie told me he'd think about it and the next day I got a call from Graham Taylor at Aston Villa, whose opening words were: 'Ron, tell me about Paul McGrath.' I probably should have said, 'Don't touch him. He's useless.' But I couldn't help myself. I told Graham what I thought and he joined Aston Villa for £450,000. The deal worked out pretty well for me because within two years I was his manager once more.

If any other Manchester United player had done off the field what Paul did, they would not have tolerated it, but because it was Paul and because they knew he had a problem, they let it go. The pain in his knee and the drink were intertwined. He used one to deal with the other.

When I became manager of Aston Villa, Gordon Cowans came up to me and said, 'Listen, gaffer, we don't mind Macca. We want him in the team.'

Eric Cantona would get the same kind of treatment at Manchester United. The players allowed him the kind of leeway they wouldn't have given anyone else at Old Trafford because instinctively they wanted his talent.

I had heard the stories about the booze and I knew he wasn't training, just playing in games, and I thought the best solution was to get rid of the problem. I'd sell him on. Liam Brady was manager of Celtic at the time and he told me he wanted to take him to Parkhead.

'Give me one-and-a-half million and he's yours.' They came back with £750,000. I was half tempted and then on a hunch said no. Whenever I watched him at Villa Park, I'd thank the Lord I'd held on to him. In the first four years of the Premier League he barely missed a game and, if you ask an Aston Villa fan who's been at the club for thirty years to name the best player they have seen, some might say Gordon Cowans but most would probably tell you it is Paul McGrath.

He didn't train; he couldn't train because his knee simply wouldn't allow it. He would come into the gym at Bodymoor Heath and just use the bikes or the static weights. He worked very closely with the Aston Villa physio, Jim Walker, and one day Jim said it would be worth increasing the load on the bike.

'It is as if you're pedalling uphill,' he said, adjusting the weight, which prompted Paul to get off.

When Jim asked why, he said, 'Well, outdoors, I always push the bike when I am going uphill.'

By the summer of 1992, I'd brought Dave Sexton into the coaching set-up at Villa and we'd gone on a pre-season tour to Germany. Paul had done virtually nothing bar sessions on the bike but we were playing Dynamo Dresden, they had a big centre-forward, Alexander Zickler, who was to play for Germany, the Premier League was beginning in a week and I thought McGrath should play.

When I told Dave he said, 'I cannot believe you are even contemplating playing him.' The first cross came in and, bang, McGrath won it. He won the second and he won the third. He scored the opening goal. Dave turned to me and said, 'I don't believe what I'm seeing.'

'You'd better believe it,' I said, 'and, what's more, he will be doing that for another forty games this season.'

Paul was on a highly incentivised contract that gave him a sizeable appearance fee, which mattered then in a way it wouldn't now. The first time I'd employed it was when I was at Sheffield Wednesday and I wanted to sign Trevor Francis.

He was 35 and had just been replaced as player-manager of Queens Park Rangers. I phoned him and said, 'Don't sit around moping, come and have a year or two with us.' He had been sacked shortly after fining Martin Allen for leaving the team hotel to attend the birth of his son, for which he had copped an enormous amount of stick. It had left him depressed and I thought he needed to relax and enjoy his football in a different environment.

I always had an affinity with Trevor because I'd marked him when he made his debut as a sixteen-year-old for Birmingham and, as I always reminded him, he had only one kick in the entire game. The kick resulted in the ball going into the back of the Oxford net, but it was still only one kick.

I'd tried to buy him for West Brom when he was at Birmingham for £650,000, and when he was at Nottingham Forest and I was at Manchester United I'd made a second fruitless attempt. That did not get past the board at Old Trafford because they were suspicious of his injury record. When I mentioned this to Trevor one night in Manchester, he became very offended and didn't talk to me for a couple of years.

Trevor's basic wage at Hillsborough wasn't great but he did have a very good incentive package, based on appearances. It might have been coincidence, but in the season and a half I had him, a footballer who had been increasingly troubled by injury played fifty league games for Sheffield Wednesday. I did the same with Des Walker in my second spell at Wednesday and I did the same with Paul McGrath. In the first two seasons of the Premier League Paul missed two games – and they were not injury related.

It is not a tactic you could use now. A couple of years ago, I was at Birmingham City and watched two brand-new Bentleys being driven into the car park by two players who had absolutely no chance of playing first-team football at St Andrew's.

When Wim Jonk was playing for Sheffield Wednesday under David Pleat, he had a contract which earned him more money if he was injured rather than if he was fit to play but dropped. If he turned out for the reserves, he would lose money. He was injured rather a lot.

Paul was at heart an intensely shy man. You would look him in the eye in the dressing room and tell him that he had to mark Alan Shearer out of the game and he'd smile and go: 'No problem.' Ask him to visit a school for a bit of publicity and he would be freaked by the idea when all he would have confronted was adoration.

Paul was worshipped in Ireland, his performances in two World Cups would see to that, and I am afraid this was the bulk of the problem. They wouldn't leave him alone, they wouldn't let him buy a drink. They would buy him a drink even on the very rare occasions he didn't want one.

Often when he went over to Dublin to play for the Republic, I sent over Jim Walker to mind him. Ireland used to play at Lansdowne Road in the afternoon and I told Jim that he and Paul were booked on the ten-past-six flight back to Birmingham and as soon as McGrath left the dressing room, he should man-mark him. 'He will probably be late because he always picks up the man-of-the-match award, but as soon as he appears get him in the car and make sure he gets to Dublin airport. If he doesn't, I'll sack you.'

Jim took his responsibilities very seriously. He had played for Derby under Brian Clough, always on the fringes of that side. I once saw a photo of the team heading off to their usual end-of-season jaunt to Majorca and Jim was the only one not wearing a club blazer. But the fact that he had been a player – and where he had been a player – meant Jim had spent plenty of time around big characters and he could handle Paul McGrath.

Sometimes, he would go to sleep in the corridor outside Paul's hotel room just so he wouldn't miss him. As the Republic's manager, Jack Charlton got the best out of McGrath on the pitch, but once the final whistle went it wasn't his problem – it was mine.

Jim would park the car by a pink-painted pub near Lansdowne Road and when the final whistle went he would make his move. Paul always made the flight to Birmingham.

The great players motivate themselves. Paul Scholes would seldom, if ever, have needed motivating during his years at Manchester United. Bryan Robson wanted paying properly, that was natural, but his chief desire was to be the best. His make-up would be little different from Steven Gerrard's.

The vast majority of footballers I have come across like discipline. They want to feel that someone is in control and that they don't have to make too many decisions for themselves, and they will accept a bollocking.

Andy Gray was my assistant during my first season at Aston Villa and we had just narrowly beaten Swindon in the fifth round of the FA Cup. Swindon were managed by Glenn Hoddle then and had run us very close, to the extent that Tony Daley had let one of their full-backs go and nearly cost us an equaliser at the death.

The draw for the quarter-finals – which saw Villa paired with Liverpool at Anfield – was straight after the final whistle. I had to go and do television interviews and comment on the draw and I told Andy to go into the dressing room and 'have a pop' at the players who had very nearly cost us the win.

By the time I came back, Andy's attempt to 'have a pop' had got completely out of hand. Tony Daley, who was a lovely kid, was looking distraught. I tried to defuse the situation – 'Yes, take that on board, Tony' – before turning to the rest of the squad and trying to calm everything down by telling them, 'We've got Liverpool next and we can do them, can't we?' (We didn't as it happened – Villa lost the quarter-final 1–0.) I turned to Andy when we were out of earshot of the rest of the squad: 'I said, "Have a go". You were a hair's-breadth from having him in tears.'

Alex Ferguson used the 'hairdryer' very sparingly. If you scream at people week-in and week-out, they will go deaf. Your words very quickly lose their meaning. But sometimes, you walk into the dressing room at half-time and it is not about tactics, you just want to steam into someone.

In September 1993, Villa were at Oldham, we were a goal down and I went into Boundary Park's tiny dressing room determined to make an impression. 'Go out there and get it sorted,' I shouted, and threw a plastic cup on the floor to reinforce the point. I didn't realise it was full of tea and as it bounced it went all over Dean Saunders, who scored five minutes after the restart and ran over to the bench and shouted, 'Brilliant trick, gaffer, brilliant.'

Sometimes, you need to relax your players so they don't think too much about what they are about to do. In 1994 we were in the Wembley dressing rooms waiting to go out for the League Cup final against Manchester United. The atmosphere was tense, everyone waiting for me to give the last few instructions.

'I have one final thing for you lads,' I said. They all looked round ready. 'What's the capital of Ecuador?' I asked. Everyone looked nonplussed and we walked out. Dean Saunders turned round and said, 'What's this all about?'

'Don't tell anybody, but the answer's Quito.'

We won the match.

# NINE

THERE ARE ONLY TWO BIG GAMES I'VE BEEN INVOLVED WITH
where I knew we were going to win long before kick-off. The 1985 FA
Cup final when Manchester United played Everton and the 1991 League
Cup final when Sheffield Wednesday faced Manchester United.

There was no obvious reason for optimism. In both finals we were
facing teams who had just won or were to win the Cup Winners' Cup.
In 1985 Everton were champions of England and attempting to become
the third club in the modern era to do the Double. Manchester United
finished sixth in the First Division and Sheffield Wednesday ended up
third in the Second Division. But as the days ran down towards Wembley,
I just knew we would win.

We stayed at the same hotel, the Oakley Court, a Victorian country
house overlooking the Thames at Windsor. However, I made sure Sheffield Wednesday's stay was very different from Manchester United's. With
United it was a straightforward game in London. We would go there,
stay a night, play the game and come home. It was business.

That Sheffield Wednesday team was full of good lads but had very
few members who had experienced the kind of pressures that come with
a cup final against Manchester United. So I decided to make it an event.

The game was on the Sunday so we travelled down from Yorkshire on the Friday morning and took the players and their wives to a good Italian restaurant in London for lunch with a few bottles of wine and then took them to the Royal Lancaster Hotel near Hyde Park.

Then at half-nine on Saturday morning, I took the players to Oakley Court and from there to a training session at Bisham Abbey. It was a much longer session than they were used to because I wanted to tire them so that on Saturday night they would sleep well.

On the day of the match, I brought Stan Boardman on to the coach as we travelled to Wembley to do his cabaret act. I wanted every member of that team to feel he was part of a special event. I wanted them to taste it and I wanted them to want to do it again.

That experience, I think, played its part in the fact that Sheffield Wednesday went to Wembley four times in the space of a few weeks in 1993. A lot of the players Trevor Francis took to two cup finals, an FA Cup semi-final against Sheffield United and an FA Cup replay, were the same ones that had been to Wembley two years before. It had given them the urge to go back.

I was never one for Churchillian speeches before a big game. I tended to be one for precise instructions. In 1991 Manchester United's outstanding performer was Lee Sharpe and on the Saturday morning at Bisham Abbey we had spent an hour or more analysing his impact.

My instructions were that if Manchester United had the ball, we should try to make them play the ball out to their right, towards Neil Webb, who was not an authentic winger. Webb was much more of a central midfielder and he hadn't the pace to really hurt us. I also wanted us to close down Paul Ince and force him to play the ball to his right, away from Sharpe. It was all about sealing off the most obvious danger.

As it happened, Lee Sharpe broke away and almost scored in the first minute of the match, but the theory worked pretty well with Roland Nilsson, a terrific pro, doing a very fine containing job on Sharpe at right-back.

The 1985 final was one of the best games I have ever managed. We were playing the champions of England who had won the title by thirteen points and who had just won the Cup Winners' Cup in Rotterdam, while Manchester United were coming to Wembley on the back of a 5–1 thrashing from Watford. We finished the game with ten men and yet when Kevin Moran was sent off with a dozen minutes remaining, I was still confident. 'We need to put Sparky on his own up front and hold out for Thursday and the replay,' Mick Brown said when Moran walked off. 'No,' I said. 'We will win this.' I moved Frank Stapleton to centre-half but pushed Norman Whiteside up to join Mark Hughes in attack. I wanted Jesper Olsen and Gordon Strachan to play as far up the pitch as they could. I trusted Bryan Robson to protect the now-makeshift back four. Norman Whiteside scored the only goal in extra time. Afterwards, their manager, Howard Kendall, claimed Everton were knackered because they had played the Cup Winners' Cup final on the Wednesday and had come to London from Holland via Liverpool. I didn't buy that. The moment Everton beat Bayern Munich in the semi-finals, they knew they were going to win the Cup Winners' Cup. Rapid Vienna, who they played in the final, were desperately ordinary.

We had endured a much harder night on the Tuesday against Watford. I knew Everton would employ Graeme Sharp and Andy Gray in attack and they would beat nobody for pace. Everton would pound it up to them and they would feed off the second ball. I did not want Gray and Sharp to spend all afternoon under our crossbar. I needed to keep them at bay. The best way to deal with them was to hold a high defensive line and I wanted to test the theory out at Vicarage Road.

The flaw in that plan was that Watford's attack was led by Luther Blissett and John Barnes, who had all the pace in the world. I walked into the dressing room and announced, 'I have to tell you, lads, we won't be playing that way on Saturday.'

Eleven days later another team from Merseyside lost another final 1–0 but nobody was much interested in the result. It was Heysel.

The deaths of 39, mostly Italian, supporters meant English club would be banned from Europe for five years. They had been the dominant force in European football for nearly a decade. Aston Villa had won the European Cup, Nottingham Forest had won it twice, Liverpool had won it four times. Tottenham, Ipswich and Liverpool had won the UEFA Cup, Everton the Cup Winners' Cup.

Between 1976 and 1985, English teams collected eleven major European trophies. In the first 23 years of the Premier League, English teams won only eight. Part of the remit of the Premier League had been to improve English clubs' performances in Europe. You tell me if it's worked.

The question that haunted us all, but particularly Howard Kendall and Everton, was how would we have done without Heysel? Whether Everton would have had enough craft to have won the European Cup, I don't know. Everton's tactics were very effective but sometimes pretty obvious.

On the other hand, bringing Gary Lineker to Goodison Park in the summer of 1985 might have given Everton the guile they required and, with the exception of Juventus, there were no great teams on the Continent. During the years of the Heysel ban Juventus did not win the European Cup, which was claimed by some very ordinary sides: Steaua Bucharest in 1986, Porto in 1987 and PSV Eindhoven in 1988. Then came the great AC Milan team, built by Arrigo Sacchi, which was to overshadow everyone.

At the start of the following season an acquaintance of mine was opening a clothes shop in Bury. He was much better friends with Howard Kendall and we both agreed to come. I brought the FA Cup and Howard took along the League Championship, the Cup Winners' Cup, the Charity Shield and his manager-of-the-year trophy. Peter Reid and Robbo came along and there was quite a party.

As it came to an end, a guy who worked as a rep for the Italian suit-makers Pal Zileri offered to take the trophies home and look after them. I have no idea why Howard and I agreed to do this – drink may have been involved – but I do recall this man putting all the silverware in the back of his Hillman Avenger and driving off into the night. After he disappeared it occurred to us both that we might have made the greatest blunder of our lives.

As it turned out, the trophies were all perfectly safe, but the one

Manchester United looked like they might be getting their hands on in the autumn of 1985 was the League Championship. By 9 November we had won thirteen and drawn two of our fifteen matches.

Then Bryan Robson was badly injured playing for England against Turkey and was out for three months. The next game, at Sheffield Wednesday, was the one where we suffered our first defeat.

Manchester United have always been more than one man but Robbo was in exceptional form. If you removed Diego Maradona from Argentina, would they have got anywhere near the 1986 World Cup?

We lost more than just Bryan. We lost Paul McGrath and Gordon Strachan, key players in key positions. And although Manchester United had put together their best ever start, we hadn't quite shaken off Liverpool. The gap was eleven points when we went to Hillsborough, when we came back it was eight and it kept on being whittled down. By 7 December we were level. Liverpool lost the Merseyside derby in February and did not lose again.

The damage done by the loss of Robson and McGrath was obvious but Strachan was a very underrated footballer, one of the best I have ever worked with. He was tricky, he was canny, he knew the game. He could pull a stroke with free-kicks curled around the box. When he was at Manchester United and Leeds, he had a trick of crouching down as the opposition formed a wall and hitting the ball from a position the goalkeeper couldn't see.

Alex Ferguson didn't want him at Aberdeen, the two men grated on each other, and I bought him for £500,000, which was a third of the fee Milan had paid for Ray Wilkins. With the rest of the money I bought Jesper Olsen and Alan Brazil.

Maybe it was a personality thing, maybe it was an error of judgement, but, like Paul McGrath, Fergie thought Strach was finished long before he was. They left Old Trafford in the same year – 1989 – McGrath to Aston Villa, Strachan to Leeds. I'd tried to get Gordon to Sheffield Wednesday but Howard Wilkinson made him the highest-paid player in the league and that was that. In 1992, Strachan won the league title with Leeds and the following year McGrath almost did with Aston Villa.

Manchester United finished fourth in 1986, twelve points behind Liverpool. The game rolled on to Mexico and the World Cup, which was where the name 'Alex Ferguson' first began to be linked with Old Trafford. It was to be a difficult tournament for Manchester United in other ways. Five of our players, including Bryan Robson, had returned home injured and Mark Hughes had left the club.

I am always asked how I could have let a 22-year-old striker who had scored seventeen league goals the previous season leave Old Trafford, but the answer is always that we had no choice. When Barcelona came in for him, contractually we did not have a leg to stand on.

Sparky had been on a junior contract, worth about £200 a week. He could leave at the end of the season for ten times the value of the contract, which would have been something like £20,000. We sorted him out with a new deal but his agent insisted on a clause that if anybody offered £2m, Manchester United would be bound to allow him to talk to them. Terry Venables was then manager of Barcelona and he knew every detail of that contract almost the moment it was signed. When Venables came calling, he knew we would have both hands tied behind our backs. Hughes would leave at the end of the 1985/86 season.

He should never have gone; he was not ready as a player or as a person – he was still very young. Sparky ended up a very highly paid recluse and his career only really started to recover when he went to Bayern Munich, where the style of football was more familiar and more people spoke English.

The consolation was that I had an agreement with the board that I could use some of that money to buy Terry Butcher. I also tried for Kerry Dixon at Chelsea but Ken Bates had put a wildly over-the-top valuation on him.

Once I learned we would have to break the British transfer record to land Dixon, I thought about bringing Cyrille Regis to Old Trafford in a swap deal for Alan Brazil, who was starting to suffer from chronic back problems.

Jim McGregor, our physio, came over to me and said, 'You have to get Brazil out of the building because in eighteen months he will be finished.' Brazil had never really settled at Old Trafford, although his goals-per-game record – eight in thirty-one – was not disastrous. He had come to United from a big club and had helped Tottenham win the UEFA Cup in 1984. When I talked to Bobby Robson about Alan, whom he had managed at Ipswich, he said Brazil was the best one-on-one finisher he had ever worked with.

If he could link up with Arnold Muhren, whom he would have played with at Portman Road, then United might have a very good trick up our sleeves. I put him in the team straight away, and that was a mistake because I played him in place of Norman Whiteside, who to the Stretford End was a cult hero. It was held against Brazil. Always.

Just before the 1985 FA Cup final, Alan had scored twice against Queens Park Rangers but didn't make the cut for Wembley. He was 25, he was watching the FA Cup final in a suit and his back was starting to go. It would have been hard for him.

My reasoning was that we were only allowed a single substitute and United were weaker defensively than they were up top. We started with Frank Stapleton and Hughes in attack but, if things went wrong, we could always push Norman up from midfield. We did not have that kind of depth in defence. I named Mike Duxbury as the twelfth man and, when Kevin Moran was sent off, Stapleton played centre-half.

I badly wanted to work with Cyrille Regis again. He was still only 27 and I thought he would have been ideally suited to Manchester United. He was at Coventry and I'd been to watch him a few times and always came away thinking, 'The big man has still got it'. I had arranged the deal but then word came through that Cyrille had been injured. He had always suffered from problems with his thigh, but this was a haematoma and it was serious. I could not recommend to the board that we replaced one chronically injured footballer with another who would arrive in Manchester unfit.

Terry Gibson became my third-choice replacement for Sparky, with

Brazil moving the other way to Coventry City. He was not a success but he had several things going for him when he arrived in January 1986. He had been on a good run of form with Tottenham and he was quick. In all my years at Old Trafford the one thing Manchester United consistently lacked was real pace up front and Terry had it. If he could get flick-ons from Frank Stapleton, he might do some serious damage. That, at least, was the theory and it went the way of so many of football's theories.

# TEN

OUR BOOTS HAD NOT BEEN LAID OUT FOR TRAINING AND there was a message for Mick Brown and me to report to Martin Edwards' office. I turned to him and said, 'I wouldn't be asking for a rise today, Mick.' I didn't, however, think we'd be sacked.

It was November 1986 and United had endured a dreadful start to the season. We had just been knocked out of the League Cup, 4–1 at Southampton, ripped apart by a young Matt Le Tissier. But I thought the situation was manageable.

I have never in my managerial career had a vote of confidence, not even from Doug Ellis when I was at Aston Villa, although he did give an interview to *Football Focus* on Saturday afternoon naming me as one of the three best managers in the country. He fired me on the Thursday.

The execution was swift. Martin used the words that have ended so many managerial careers: 'We need to make a change.' He told me to see his secretary. She would sort out the details of my contract.

My attitude to it was '*que sera, sera*'. I didn't try to argue the point but I did ask if I could keep using the Cliff for the football team I used to run on a Friday night, which left Martin nonplussed.

We had a team that used to play Friday night games on the Astroturf at the Cliff. I brought in people like Joe Royle, Stuart Pearson or Willie Morgan and borrowed one of the apprentice goalies who would either be Gary Walsh or Fraser Digby. Mike Summerbee would occasionally have a game as would Frank Worthington.

Phil Black, a Manchester lad who became a football agent, would find sides for us to play against. The teams we faced always had the advantage of youth but while they ran around like lunatics all we would do was pass and pass again. The team rule was, 'nobody runs faster than the ball.'

Martin did allow us to play on for a couple of weeks but, inevitably, we were moved on and ended up staging our games on the Astroturf at Oldham.

I felt I had done the job Martin had brought me in to do. He asked me to re-establish Manchester United as a force in the English game. From 1968 to 1981 they had finished in the top four twice – which was scandalous for a club of its stature. The top four had no real meaning then and anyway English clubs were banned from Europe. But Manchester United had finished no lower than fourth in my time at Old Trafford and won the FA Cup twice.

I was aware of the talk about Alex Ferguson and Old Trafford that was swirling around Mexico during the World Cup and I knew, too, that Bobby Charlton, who was on the United board, was a fan of his. But in the summer I pressed on with the task of trying to sign Terry Butcher, who had just suffered relegation with Ipswich.

After the World Cup there was a game between the Best of Europe against the Best of South America and Gordon Strachan found himself rooming with Butcher. I got a call from Strach saying, 'I am having fish and chips with Terry and he is desperate to come to United.' I told Gordon I would work on it with the board.

Board meetings at Manchester United consisted of endless discussions about the basketball team the club was then running and about ten minutes on football. I knew by then that Bobby had sounded Fergie out about taking over – Lawrie McMenemy had told me.

I said, 'Before we go anywhere, gentlemen, what about the Terry

Butcher scenario? He would cost £750,000 and I know Tottenham are interested.'

'I don't think he is any better than what we've got,' said Bobby.

'I don't care who is the manager of this football club, be it me, Terry Venables, Graham Taylor, Howard Kendall . . .' and I paused. 'Or Alex Ferguson. They are not going to object to having Paul McGrath and Terry Butcher as their central defenders.'

'Actually,' said Martin, 'he is a good player but the trouble is that we have allocated the money for the museum.'

'Well that will be handy when we're three down,' I said. 'I'll bring the museum up for a corner.'

One of the first things Ferguson said when he came to Old Trafford was that it was a disgrace United had failed to sign Terry Butcher. One of my men, who was still on the inside, turned round and said, 'Tell your mate, he was the one who blocked it.'

It was my first sacking but I wasn't crushed by it as I think it crushed David Moyes, whom I felt was hard done by. He had been given a six-year contract and told to rebuild Manchester United and he ought to have had confidence in that contract.

What undermined him was he and the club continually stressing they were 'in transition'. They were league champions. How you go from being league champions to being 'in transition' in the space of a couple of months is something United have never satisfactorily explained. Manchester United are one of the four biggest clubs in the world. You never hear Barcelona or Bayern Munich announcing they are in transition. They cannot afford to be. They have to keep winning.

Three seasons after Alex Ferguson's departure it would be hard to argue that Manchester United are not in transition. The problems that beset them stemmed from what I would call 'chocolate factory shopping'. They bought players they took a fancy to and then wondered if they could make a team from them.

Buying Bastian Schweinsteiger made sense but not if you had already paid £28m for Morgan Schneiderlin, who played in the same position.

They also kept Michael Carrick in central midfield and, while being a very efficient footballer, he was never at his best against the highest class of player – Fergie was a hair's breadth from getting rid of him when he allowed Barcelona to run wild during the 2009 Champions League final.

Louis van Gaal might have experimented with playing Schweinsteiger as a right-sided midfielder – not a winger – which was where he started his career in Munich, but instead United found themselves with three footballers who did almost identical jobs.

On 6 November 1986 nobody talked about clubs like Manchester United being 'in transition', they were just having a bad season.

From Old Trafford, I drove back to the Cliff to invite the players back to my home in Rochdale for a farewell party. Gordon Strachan was not a drinker but the party went on all night and when he tried to drive home to the other side of Manchester, his car passed a football ground and he wondered how he had managed to get to Maine Road. He hadn't. He had driven to Leeds. He was outside Elland Road.

That night, with all the lads around me and the laughter bubbling away, I got a call from Madrid. The president of Atletico, Vicente Calderon, wanted to speak to me about becoming their manager at the end of the season. I would be taking over from Luis Aragones.

I could relax, do a bit of television work and turn down Blackburn's offer to replace Bobby Saxton as manager. In March 1987, Calderon died of a heart attack, which triggered new presidential elections.

I was asked to travel over to Madrid to support the establishment candidate and also asked, bizarrely, if I could bring along an English international to do some publicity. The only one I could get hold of was Ricky Hill, who was then at Luton, and I asked him if he fancied a trip to Spain.

Compared to what the other candidate was doing, the sight of Ricky Hill was unlikely to sway many of Atletico's voters. Jesus Gil was campaigning hard. The best way to describe him is that he looked like Private Doberman from *Sergeant Bilko*, only whereas the original Doberman was small, Gil was a giant, standing six foot six. I came to call him Mad Max.

He was mayor of Marbella and ran it as if it was his own property and as a firm supporter of General Franco his politics were, shall we say, uncompromising.

Atletico had reached the final of the Copa del Rey and would face Real Sociedad, who were then managed by John Toshack, in the final in Zaragoza. Gil paid for private trains to ferry the Atletico supporters the 240 miles to La Romareda. He also brought along Paulo Futre, who had just won the European Cup with Porto and been runner-up to Ruud Gullit in the poll to become European Footballer of the Year.

I am afraid Ricky found himself a little overshadowed. Gil won the election and appointed Cesar Menotti, who had managed Barcelona when Manchester United knocked them out of the Cup Winners' Cup, but whose great claim to fame was that he had taken Argentina to the World Cup in 1978.

While all this was going on I'd had a conversation with Brian Boundy, one of my old directors at West Bromwich Albion who had been a big supporter of mine when I was at the Hawthorns. When we talked they were bumping along the bottom of the old Second Division and he was desperate to bring the club back to what it was. He told me that he would bring in new investment, adding, 'If we don't, we will get relegated into the Third Division.' They scrambled three points clear of the relegation zone and by September 1987, realising I was unlikely to be offered the Atletico Madrid job, I agreed to come back.

Things had become desperate off the field, too. West Brom was unrecognisable from the club I had left to join Manchester United six years before. There were still some members of the old board left but any money was long gone. I once did an after-dinner speech for a hotel company on the premise that West Brom could use one of their hotels for an away game.

It was a long and very hard season. When I arrived at the Hawthorns to replace Ron Saunders, West Brom were once more bottom of the Second Division with one point from four matches – and they had also been knocked out of the League Cup by Walsall.

My first game was against Shrewsbury and we won thanks to an own-goal from Nigel Pearson, who was to become my captain at Sheffield Wednesday. I knew we had to rebuild the club quickly. I took Andy Gray from Aston Villa for £20,000, we got Brian Talbot on a free from Stoke and Kenny Swain on loan from Portsmouth, and Tony Morley, who had won the European Cup with Aston Villa but was now playing for Den Haag in Holland.

These players had all long since celebrated their thirtieth birthday and the team had a *Dad's Army* quality to it but it also had plenty of professionalism, something West Brom then lacked. There were one or two young players like David Burrows and Carlton Palmer who learned from being next to these old pros and whose careers benefited from it.

However, by the time we played Shrewsbury again, this time at Gay Meadow, we had won one game in three months. Our chairman was now Sid Lucas, the old Brummie who had welcomed me to the Hawthorns the first time around with a rather lesser car than the one I was driving at Cambridge United.

We were winning 1–0 at Shrewsbury but Sid suddenly announced he couldn't take any more and was going to sit in the dressing room until the final whistle. When the final whistle went, we had held on to the lead but, as we walked down the tunnel, I turned to Tony Morley and said, 'Watch this.' I began shouting, 'How can the referee have given it. The penalty could mean relegation.' Sid burst open the dressing-room door, his face a picture of pain, pleading to know what had happened. I pointed to the rest of the lads clattering down the tunnel and said, 'No problem, Sid. We won.' The Football League was then experimenting with relegation play-offs, an experience West Brom avoided by a single point.

By the time my second season at the Hawthorns got under way, I felt I was getting to grips with West Brom but, out of nowhere, I got a call from Jesus Gil's people. He wanted me to go to Atletico Madrid after all.

Atletico had finished third in La Liga in 1988, which had not been enough to keep Menotti his job. His replacement, Jose Ufarte, had lasted precisely three games before quitting. Job security would not be high

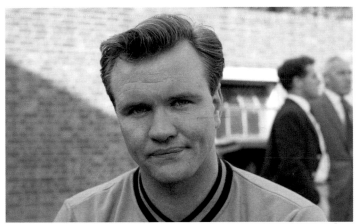

My playing career began at Oxford United. Here I am aged 23 at the start of the 1962/63 season, Oxford's first season in the Football League. *(PA)*

Somewhere in this mass of supporters, you can see me getting carried off the pitch after Oxford knocked Blackburn Rovers out of the FA Cup in the fifth round, the furthest in the competition the club has ever reached. *(PA)*

As Oxford's captain it was my duty to lead the team out in front of an expectant Manor Ground crowd. *(PA)*

Kettering Town and Cambridge United were great times but being appointed at West Brom was my most important break in management. This was taken in the summer of 1978 ahead of my first full season in charge at the Hawthorns. *(PA)*

At Heathrow Airport following the end of an eye-opening post season tour to China with West Bromwich Albion. Mick Martin, Bryan Robson and Ally Brown are also pictured. *(PA)*

Willie Johnston tested positive for a banned stimulant at the 1978 World Cup in Argentina. I met him at Heathrow Airport on his return to Britain. *(PA)*

The Bell's Whisky manager of the month for February 1983. Finals in the Milk Cup and FA Cup awaited. Everton were beaten immediately after this presentation. *(Mirrorpix)*

A trio of international players that I hoped would propel United to the next level in the 1984/85 season. A Dane in Jesper Olsen and two Scots, Alan Brazil and Gordon Strachan. *(Mirrorpix)*

Tracksuit, flip-flops and feet up. A rare let-up at Manchester United Cliff training ground in October 1984. *(Mirrorpix)*

Glory, glory Man United: winning the FA Cup at Wembley with a 1-0 victory over First Division champions Everton in 1985. *(PA)*

Two months away from the sack at Manchester United. Mounting pressure. September, 1986. *(Mirrorpix)*

Back at the Hawthorns after returning to management with West Brom. The club had fallen on hard times since my first spell there. *(PA)*

Sharing a joke with Jesús Gil y Gil, the volcanic president of Atlético Madrid, before being appointed to the Spanish club in 1988. Our working relationship didn't last too long. *(PA)*

Winning the Rumbelows Cup with Sheffield Wednesday at Wembley in 1991. My old club Manchester United were the opponents. I consider Roland Nilsson, pictured here, as one of my best buys. *(PA)*

Doug Ellis, Aston Villa's legendary chairman. He was as tough and demanding as they come. *(PA)*

Dean Saunders was an important signing for Aston Villa. He didn't really want to leave Liverpool. But I persuaded him to do so, even though the deal dragged on. *(PA)*

Relief! Beating Tranmere Rovers in the semi final of the Coca Cola Cup in 1994. We needed two legs, extra time and penalties to do it. Manchester United were beaten in the final a few weeks later. *(PA)*

Winning the League Cup again – beating United in the final again! Dalian Atkinson was one of the scorers at Wembley. *(PA)*

Another job, another Midland club. This time the brief at Coventry City in 1995 was simple: avoid relegation. *(PA)*

Under pressure: another missed chance against Leeds United at Highfield Road as the season nears its conclusion. Fortunately, we stayed up. *(PA)*

Back to Sheffield and back to Hillsborough in 1997. The fans seemed quite happy with my re-appointment at Wednesday. And so was I. *(PA)*

The job at the City Ground with Nottingham Forest was hard enough, with the team rooted to the bottom of the Premier League table. In Pierre van Hooijdonk, the club had a talented but temperamental striker. *(PA)*

In position with the wonderful Brian Moore working for ITV in 1996. I loved working as a football commentator. *(PA)*

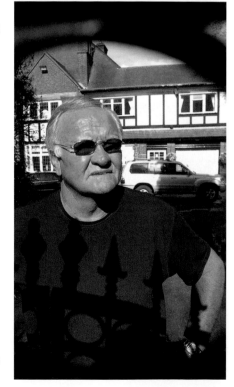

A huge mistake. Something I regret. After making an off-air remark about Marcel Desailly, I decided to resign from ITV. The press were waiting for me the next morning. *(PA)*

At home in Worcestershire during my first spell as manager of West Brom. Maggie and I are big dog lovers. *(Mirrorpix)*

This was taken a few weeks after I took charge at Coventry City. The job meant I didn't have to move home. *(Mirrorpix)*

As manager of Sheffield Wednesday – back in the city I called 'Rome' because of its seven hills, I commuted most days from Worcestershire. *(PA)*

Love and success. Maggie and I leaving London for Manchester in the wake of FA Cup glory in 1985. *(Mirrorpix)*

and West Brom were climbing the table and looking like they might be on an upward curve.

The club had a new chairman, John Silk, and I went to him and told him that if he put another eighteen months on my existing contract I thought I could get them promoted to the First Division. The subject of money never came up and I wasn't after a raise. Silk replied, 'Get us out of this division and we will look at your contract.'

I was on a £40,000 salary at the Hawthorns. Atletico Madrid were offering a quarter of a million a year. They were playing in the top division in Spain. In Paulo Futre they employed one of the best footballers in Europe. Maybe I could handle the president.

Brian Talbot took over as player/manager and West Brom did quite well for a while. However, the rot set in and in January 1991 they were knocked out of the FA Cup at home to Woking. Brian was replaced by Bobby Gould, who did what I had promised John Silk in the autumn of 1988. He took West Brom out of the Second Division and was given a contract extension. He had relegated them.

# ELEVEN

WATCHING HIM IN THE DIRECTORS' BOX, STRUTTING BACK-
wards and forwards, I thought standing next to Jesus Gil must have been
the nearest thing to hanging out with Benito Mussolini. He would turn
up to the ground with his own private army, recruited from his adopted
home town of Marbella, some of whom would sing songs dedicated to
him. Mad Max was the archetypal football dictator. Curiously, I never
actually had a stand-up argument with him.

Atletico was not the first opportunity I had of managing in Spain.
In 1984 I'd been approached by Barcelona shortly after Manchester
United had knocked them out of the Cup Winners' Cup. This was also
to replace Cesar Menotti.

I wasn't the only English candidate. They had sounded out Bobby
Robson, who was then managing England, a position he felt he could
not leave. Then I had a call from Terry Venables, who was managing
Crystal Palace. He wanted a video of our tie against Barcelona. Barca
and their president, Josep Nunez, were desperate for an English manager
and now there was another candidate.

The first stumbling block had been the contract. I'd wanted three
years but Barcelona were only prepared to offer two. I met them in
London, at the Royal Lancaster Hotel. Joe Melling, one of my best

journalistic contacts, sat in on the talks.

I had known Joe since I first started out with West Bromwich Albion, when I was living in the Europa Hotel. Joe had moved down to cover Midlands football for the *Daily Express* and Jim Smith had also moved down from Blackburn to manage Birmingham. All three of us were living in hotels. When we needed to get out of our rooms, we would pal up.

Nunez was close to Robson and when Bobby turned down the job, he asked him for some advice. Bobby told him that while Terry was genuinely interested in going to Catalonia, I was probably using the situation to get a better deal from Manchester United. That was absolutely not the case. When Joe met Bobby later he mentioned it and Bobby said, 'I think I may have cost Ron the Barcelona job.' I rather think he did.

Four years later, I was ready to go to Spain. I had met Maggie, my second wife, who spoke Spanish, and I was very keen to learn. I was given a translator, Manolo, a member of the vast entourage Mad Max kept around him.

One of our first games was against Osasuna, who had two former Liverpool players: Michael Robinson, who I considered to be past his best at that stage of his career, and Sammy Lee. They proceeded to murder us. It convinced me that one of the qualifications to play centre-half in Spain was an inability to head the ball.

At half-time I tried to explain to my centre-backs that I wanted them to head the ball. Manolo said in his sing-song Spanish, 'Mister would like it very much if you would head the ball, please.' I pushed him out of the way, grabbed the two centre-backs by the shirt and screamed, '*Quiero que el balon de mierda la cabeza. Si!*'

Mad Max liked to join us on the coach when we made the short trips to home games and he would ask for the referees' list. The shout would come up: '*Arbitro?*' and we would tell him. Just before the derby with Real Madrid the usual question came up from Gil: '*Arbitro?*' and then, once we told him, there was a pause and then: '*Problema!*'

Jesus Gil's way of dealing with a problem was to charge at it head on, going straight to the press to list all the favours Real had ever had from referees. In the run-up to the derby he had bitterly attacked the Real Madrid president, Ramon Mendoza, calling him 'a man who would break into my ranch and steal my horses'.

As a result, Mendoza had him banned from the Bernabeu. Mad Max then appeared on the front page of the Spanish sports paper *Marca* dressed in a convict's uniform, gripping a set of prison bars. He then gave a press conference saying that if he wasn't allowed in Atletico would send their juniors to contest the derby. I then had to go to the journalists and brief them that this was one thing we absolutely would not be doing.

Saturday night in the Bernabeu was one of the experiences of a lifetime. The Bernabeu in 1988 would not have passed a health and safety inspection. Glancing round the exposed concrete, I kept thinking that this place would fall down, sooner rather than later.

It was the atmosphere that made the stadium. As I walked out of the tunnel in my overcoat to protect me against the winter chill, there were suddenly shouts of *'Ingles, Ingles!'* everywhere. I drank it in.

It was an astonishing match. The derby ended with Atletico down to nine men and Real with ten. Mad Max had installed himself in a television studio and rang me from there at half-time. Paulo Futre was one of those dismissed but, in spite of it all, we had four one-on-ones that saw our forwards cleaned out by the Real keeper, Francisco Buyo, in a way Toni Schumacher might have recognised. We lost 2-1 and Real's winner arrived in the 97th minute. To call it a dodgy decision would have been a vast understatement.

The press room in the Bernabeu was jammed and everyone there expected a condemnation of the referee. I replied in my best Spanish, *'En Inglaterra nunca criticamos el arbitro.'* The headline in the next day's *Marca* was: 'English gentleman refuses to attack the referee.'

The team bus dropped me off in the centre of Madrid so I could see some friends who had travelled out for the game. It then proceeded to the Calderon stadium, where Gil was waiting, and as they stepped out of the coach he gave everyone a bundle of notes.

Atletico had a fantastic team, players I loved working with. There was Paulo Futre, of course, who was a joy to coach. On the Friday, before every match, we would have a three-touch game. I'd shout, *'Veinte minutos – tres toques.'* He would shake his head and go, *'No, Mister, no. Libre!'* He wanted to dribble everywhere.

We had Abel Resino in goal, who would go on to manage Atletico Madrid twenty years after I'd left. At right-back there was Tomas, a fabulous defender who played international football for Spain, and Donato, a centre-back who was still playing football for Deportivo La Coruna in his forties. He was a Brazilian, born in Rio de Janeiro, and became a Spanish citizen when he married a local girl. I remembered Donato when I was trying to get Mark Bosnich to play for Aston Villa.

Bosnich had joined Manchester United in 1989, when he was seventeen, and played a few games for them when he was still officially a student. But when that stopped, United couldn't get a work permit for him. Alex Ferguson tried to persuade him to go to Holland or Denmark on loan, an idea Bosnich turned down flat, and he went back to Sydney.

When I was managing Aston Villa, our first-choice keeper was Nigel Spink, we had a good young lad called Michael Oakes, but we'd lost our middle keeper, Lee Butler, who'd gone to Barnsley.

I got a call from Graham Smith, who had been my keeper at Cambridge and who was now working for Adidas. He said he could get me Mark Bosnich. I said, 'You'll never get a work permit for him.' Graham said he knew a lawyer in Hong Kong who could sort most things. But even he would find getting the Home Office to agree a work permit for Bosnich something of a problem. Then I said, remembering Donato, 'Does he have a girlfriend?'

He had one, they were genuinely a couple and she lived in Manchester. I said to Graham, 'Well, why doesn't he marry her?' He married Laura and Mark joined Aston Villa, although the marriage didn't last.

I thought the Madrid derby was a turning point in my time at Atletico. They may have lost but they had performed heroically; some of the players were in tears in the dressing room. On the Monday, I took the players out for a meal in a Basque restaurant at the heart of the old city.

It hadn't been my intention to invite the president but Mad Max turned up and gave a long, rambling speech in which he said we had taken the spirit of Atletico Madrid to new levels. He left and asked if I could pick up the bill, although given what he'd just said about me, I felt I could afford it. He fired me about three weeks later.

It could not have been because of the results. We beat Murcia and then went to Valladolid, who had not lost at the Jose Zorrilla stadium all season. We beat them, drew with Celta Vigo and then, with La Liga having a fortnight's break, I went home to sort out a few things. Atletico Madrid were fourth bottom when I arrived with my assistant, Colin Addison, who I'd worked with at West Brom and who had previously had success getting Celta Vigo promoted.

We were now fourth in La Liga, a few points behind Real Madrid, we were in the quarter-finals of the Copa del Rey; there was nothing at all to suggest what would happen next.

Just before we were due to play Celta Vigo, we had a meeting in the president's office in the centre of Madrid. Before we sat down, Manolo, the translator, turned to me and said, 'The president would like to ask you a favour, Ron, but he is too shy to ask you himself.'

Shyness was an affliction Jesus Gil had kept well hidden during my time in Madrid. Before I'd arrived to take up my post, Gil had sacked four players, including the club captain Juan Arteche, who had played more than 300 times for Atletico. He had also fired the club doctor who had been with the team for 24 years.

The doctor had responded by taking them to a tribunal, which was due on Monday. Manolo said, 'Could you play Andoni Goikoetxea on Sunday?' The man known as the Butcher of Bilbao for his crippling of Diego Maradona had a broken leg. He couldn't even limp.

'Are you serious?'

Manolo was insistent: 'The thing is that on Monday the doctor will tell the tribunal that it is his professional opinion that Goikoetxea will never play again and that is why Senor Gil dismissed him from the club. If you could play him on Sunday, it will help our legal case.'

'I'll tell you what I'll do. I will put him on the bench and he can try to limp up and down that touchline if he wants to prove a point, but I can tell you now he has absolutely no chance of coming on.'

We battered Celta Vigo, we should have won comfortably, but they managed to cling on for a point and the next day, the day of the tribunal, I flew home. I also wanted to check out two players who I thought Atletico Madrid should be after.

Mad Max had been contacted by Silvio Berlusconi at AC Milan, who was offering him £6m for Paulo Futre. Gil had asked me, 'If you had the money, what would you do with it?'

I told him I would buy two German footballers, Thomas Hassler, who was then playing for Cologne, and Jurgen Klinsmann, who had been voted the Bundesliga's player of the year in 1988 and was then driving Stuttgart towards a UEFA Cup final. I added that I would offer Manchester United £1m for Bryan Robson and, at that stage of his career, I thought Alex Ferguson would cut a deal. Robbo was coming up to 32 then but playing one game a week he would have romped Spain. I told the president he could buy those three and still have change from Futre.

On the Monday night, back in England, I received a call from Colin Addison.

'Ron, I am ringing you to let you know that they have offered me your job.'

'Really, how did you leave it, Col?'

'They've offered me the same money.'

'So you've talked terms with them?'

'Sort of.'

I had heard nothing from the club but I managed to arrange a meeting with them on the Thursday. Birmingham airport, at six o'clock on a dark February morning, was smothered in fog. I got a car to take me to Heathrow. More fog. I waited for hours in departures before I took a call from Dennis Roach, who was acting as my agent in Spain.

'Ron, don't bother. It's like a madhouse over here. There are cameramen everywhere and I can't make any sense of what's going on.'

I never went back to Madrid, never took charge of another match at the Vicente Calderon. Colin took over and, though it might seem from a distance that he had stabbed me in the back, he hadn't. We were living on a volcano, we all knew it would go off and, when it did, we knew we would have to make the best of it.

I did think that when Colin was offered my job he could have said, 'I'll take it when you've sorted Ron's contract out.' However, with Jesus Gil that may have been easier said than done. Conversations with Mad Max tended to be one-way streets. Colin took Atletico to the semi-finals of the Copa del Rey, where once more they played and lost to Real Madrid. He was sacked during the half-time interval.

On the Saturday, I took myself off to watch Aston Villa beat Sheffield Wednesday. On my way out of Villa Park, I was buttonholed by one of the Wednesday directors, who asked me what I was doing there.

I told him what had happened in Madrid and on the Monday I got a call from Sheffield Wednesday asking if I'd be interested in the manager's job. I told them that Atletico had not yet settled my contract and I couldn't be seen to be talking to another club while that was going on, unless they would indemnify me in case I was not given any compensation.

When I eventually went to Spain for the tribunal, Atletico Madrid tried to argue that I had resigned to join another English club.

I wanted to stay in Spain. I had offers from Valencia and Seville, while Sheffield Wednesday were in desperate trouble. They had won one league game in almost four months. The plan I cobbled together was to go to Hillsborough, try to keep them up, and then return to Spain. In the end, I stayed at Sheffield Wednesday for two-and-a-half years.

Madrid was like being in a movie. Everything about the job was a story. There were press conferences after every training session. When I dented my club car, a modest Peugeot that was referred to as my 'limousine', it merited a page lead in *Marca*. When we had five-a-sides, I used to award a yellow jersey to whoever had played the worst. Each dishing out of the yellow jersey was faithfully reported by *Marca*.

When I first came to the club, the dressing room at the Vicente Calderon just before kick-off would be full of celebrities, the president's cronies and anybody else who fancied pushing their head around the door. This had to stop. When the players went to warm up, 45 minutes before kick-off, I found one big old bruiser who looked like he had fought with Franco in the Revolution and who had in fact played centre-half for Madrid in the 1940s and 50s. I told him to stand by the dressing-room door and let nobody in. He did just that, arms folded outside the door, glowering with menace.

To me, Madrid was full of stardust, though when you went out in the evenings you were left alone, treated with respect, which might not be the case now. If you were a footballer in Madrid, you could spend all day after training with a woman and nobody would mind. Make a bad pass in a five-a-side and they would analyse it to death. Drink before a game and they would hate you for it.

We had one fairly ordinary player, Sergio Marrero, who'd come to Madrid from Las Palmas in the Canary Islands. One day he had been spotted in a bar, drinking whisky. I had no idea what had happened but when I went into training I could sense a stigma around him. The club secretary, a smashing old boy called Carlos Pena, came over, pointed and said, 'Mister, he's been drinking.' The rest of the team had cut him dead.

On New Year's Day we were due to play Barcelona in an evening kick-off and, naturally, I had arranged for the team to spend the night before in a hotel where we could monitor them.

Atletico employed a masseur who I liked spending time with because he spoke the clearest, most beautiful Castilian Spanish. He came over to me and said, 'Why don't you let them go home to their families? They will have their New Year's Eve meal with their families, they will see the new year in and then they will return to the hotel.'

It was a request I would not even have contemplated in England. The carnage that would come from allowing a group of footballers out on New Year's Eve would have been all too predictable. I agreed and at one in the morning every one of my team was back at the hotel. They had had one glass of champagne or *cava*, they had their dozen grapes, one for each chime of the clock as it struck midnight, and then they had left.

What English footballers might have done, I shudder to think, but by way of contrast the Barcelona team were staying in the same hotel as I was living in and that evening Gary Lineker and Francisco Carrasco were in the bar and they were both slaughtering Johan Cruyff, who was in his first season as Barcelona manager and who had been playing Gary on the right wing. He would play him as centre-forward the next day and Gary would score.

Spanish footballers didn't drink but they loved to eat. We usually flew to away games but for Osasuna, who are based in Pamplona, 250 miles north of Madrid, we took a coach. We finished training at one, were on the coach after lunch at two and were due to check into the hotel and have a meal at six. Suddenly, I heard from the back of the bus, '*Mister, Mister, Comida!*' We stopped at a roadside café for baguettes.

Once, I found myself with Maggie walking down the Calle de Serrano, which is Madrid's Bond Street. On the other side, I saw Seve Ballesteros and I ran over the road shouting, 'Seve, Seve,' and shook hands with him.

This was 1988, he had just won the Open for the third time. He was the most famous and charismatic golfer in the world and after training I told the players I'd met him in Madrid. Most of them hadn't a clue who Ballesteros was.

On the fifth anniversary of my sacking at Manchester United, Atletico Madrid played Manchester United at Old Trafford, knocking them out of the Cup Winners' Cup. I was doing commentary for television, Paulo Futre and Tomas had got to hear about it and they wouldn't let the coach leave until they'd found me.

I was chatting to them when, out of the corner of my eye, I caught a familiar shape looming towards me. It was Mad Max. 'Ah,' he boomed. 'My favourite enemy!'

Paulo did eventually get his move to Serie A, where they slashed him to pieces. He joined not Milan but Reggiana, who had just been promoted. On his debut he scored in the first half and had his leg broken in the second. He never really recovered from the injury and although he was transferred to Milan, he spent most of his time on the bench or in the San Siro's stands. They had no use for him.

Harry Redknapp took a punt and brought him to West Ham. I was with Coventry then and we were staying in a hotel in Waltham Abbey before playing a night match at Upton Park. We'd had lunch, the players had gone to bed and I was sitting with Noel Whelan, who was injured and wouldn't be involved.

Suddenly, Paulo came in. He was staying at the same hotel. He came across, hugged me and I introduced him to Noel. Paulo knew about Noel's career, knew he had come to us from Leeds, but I am not sure Noel Whelan knew anything about Paulo Futre.

The last time I came across Mad Max was when I was managing Aston Villa. We took part in a pre-season tournament at Santiago de Compostela in the north of Spain and beat Atletico Madrid in the final.

Atletico were then managed by Francisco Maturana, who had just had the experience of taking Colombia to the 1994 World Cup, which had ended with the assassination of their centre-half, Andres Escobar. He then had the experience of being sacked by Jesus Gil for losing a pre-season tournament.

He was reinstated and lasted nine more games before the end came.

In all, Gil fired seventeen managers in seven years before Raddy Antic brought some stability to the club and won them the Double in 1996, which Gil celebrated by parading through Madrid on the back of an elephant.

Mad Max was eventually laid low by a corruption scandal but he was, in his way, an impressive character who filled every room he ever stood in. He was very close to Lola Flores, who was one of Spain's great flamenco singers and the aunt of Quique Sanchez Flores who would go on to manage Atletico and Watford. The singer and the president are buried near each other in the Cemetery of Our Lady of Almudena.

# TWELVE

IT WAS SHEFFIELD WEDNESDAY'S END-OF-SEASON DINNER, AN
occasion when fans spend a lot of money to mingle with the players,
discuss the year just gone and reminisce, usually with a glass in their hand.

The trouble was that I and the players they were paying so much to
mingle with had, that afternoon, just relegated the club. We were not
expecting to be bought too many rounds of drinks.

May 1990 was the first time I had relegated anyone and nobody at
Hillsborough saw it coming. On 31 March we were playing Tottenham
at home. Wednesday were thirteenth in Division One with forty points
and, if we won, we would be a few points off fifth place. We could also go
twelve points clear of the relegation zone, although none of us thought
that was particularly significant.

We were comfortable, Trevor Francis had scored two and then came
off injured and in the time it took to get him off the pitch and into the
dressing rooms Gary Lineker had scored twice and we lost 4–2.

Of the remaining five games, Sheffield Wednesday won just one and
lost all the others, but the alarm bells never sounded because we were
playing so well. If we had been struggling I might have been more alert
to what was going on but we went to Queens Park Rangers, struck the
woodwork repeatedly and lost 1–0. We went to Maine Road, played

Manchester City off the park and lost 2–1. It was some of the best football Sheffield Wednesday had played all season. We nicked a win at Charlton which meant that, going into the final game of the season, we had 43 points, two fewer than Manchester United, who were in sixteenth position, and three more than Luton, who were in the final relegation position. Our goal difference was two better. We were at home to Nottingham Forest, Luton, who had won one away game all season, were at Derby. It would take something to send us down. Something happened.

Luton won 3–2 at the Baseball Ground. We lost 3–0 at home to Forest and went down on goal difference with 43 points. As we walked off, it wasn't clear whether we were relegated at all. At the end of the game there had been a report that Derby had equalised, which led to me being photographed punching the air, but, like so many rumours on the final day, it turned out to be false. We had been relegated and a little lad came up to me crying his eyes out.

Emlyn Hughes, who lived in Sheffield, had travelled with us on the team bus from the hotel and said to me, 'I cannot believe it. I didn't get a single impression from being with those lads that they expected to go down.'

I told the team that, whatever they felt, they would be attending the end-of-season dinner and then we would go on an end-of-season trip to Majorca, where by chance we ran into the entire Luton team, who were doing exactly the same thing, albeit with rather more to celebrate.

We walked into the room, fearing the worst, and then the fans began clapping us. It was something I never expected, it was humbling. 'I tell you now,' I told them. 'We will put this right next season.'

The one thing I will always remember about Sheffield Wednesday are the fans. Howard Wilkinson had done very well at Hillsborough in a very functional way. My style was rather different. I wanted Wednesday to play with a bit of flair and the fans, I think, appreciated that.

What they didn't know was that I had been offered the Aston Villa job. Graham Taylor had come to see me and said he was to become the next England manager after the World Cup in Italy and would I be interested in replacing him?

'I don't see how I can, Graham,' was the answer. 'I have just got relegated. I can't walk out now.'

Instead, I got the Sheffield Wednesday lads together and said, 'Let's see if we can't bounce back in one. We are good enough. I will try to keep this squad together.'

Before we were relegated, Real Sociedad had been interested in Franz Carr, who was on loan from Nottingham Forest. In March they had sent Luis Arconada, who was coming to the end of a fifteen-year stint as their goalkeeper, to Hillsborough to watch us beat Manchester United 1–0, where Dalian Atkinson played an absolute blinder. They shifted their attention from Carr to Atkinson. We sold Dalian for £1.5m. I used some of the money to bring in Danny Wilson from Luton.

In 1990 it was easier then to go straight back up than it was to become. The players in the top division were well paid but they were not on millionaire wages. There was not the desperate requirement to slash and burn that was to engulf teams relegated from the Premier League.

I liken it to what happened to Burnley when they went down in 2015. They were not financially over-extended, they had not lashed out on stupid wages and, apart from Kieran Trippier, whom they sold to Tottenham, Sean Dyche was able to keep his squad together.

When Birmingham went down in 2011, a month after winning the League Cup, the board at St Andrew's decided to asset-strip the club. The Birmingham side Alex McLeish had constructed was perfectly capable of going straight back up, had the owners held their nerve, but they cracked and the result was that they languished in the Championship.

The worry for me was that, although I knew this Sheffield Wednesday team was good enough to be a top-half side in the old First Division, I wondered if they could stick it out lower down. I needn't have worried. We won five of our first six games, beating Ipswich 2–0 at Portman Road, putting five past Hull at Hillsborough and beating Leicester 4–2 at Filbert Street. David Pleat, who was managing Leicester, said Sheffield Wednesday were the 'best passing team I have seen in this division,' which was a real source of encouragement.

Had we not become involved in the League Cup, I think Wednesday would have ended the seasons as champions. We went up in third place behind Oldham and West Ham. The mantra that sides aiming for promotion or trying to stay in the Premier League should aim to be eliminated from cup competitions at the first opportunity is an argument I have never begun to understand. Football supporters crave silverware, they long for the big days out. It is what they pay their money for.

Just before Birmingham went to Wembley to play Arsenal in the League Cup final, I was playing golf with some of their fans and I asked them, 'What would you prefer? Get beat on Sunday and survive, or win the cup and go down?' They wanted the cup, because it would be a day they would always have. It was the same at Wigan. In Sunderland they still talk of 1973.

It is more than a quarter of a century since Sheffield Wednesday beat Manchester United at Wembley but it is still a vivid part of the club. All my pre-match preparations were about relaxing the team, which is why our coach from Bisham Abbey to Wembley contained Stan Boardman.

He did his stand-up routine on the bus and, as we turned into Wembley Way, we were confronted by a mass of blue and white. Manchester United had been there so many times over the years that they might have become blasé about it all but in Sheffield it was an enormous deal.

Stan stood up, grabbed the microphone, and said, 'You see this lot. They have all cashed in their giros, spent every penny they have, to come down here and you are not going to let them down.'

Whenever I stood in the tunnel at Wembley, I used to have a ritual of having a brandy in a little paper cup. Some of my old backroom staff like Brian Whitehouse, who was the reserve-team manager, and Eric Harrison were still with Manchester United and I offered them the cup.

I offered it to Alex Ferguson, who stared at me as if I was trying to get him to drink poison. He was, in 1991, still very uptight and very much under pressure. A few years later, I think he would have joined me in a drink.

I tended to get on OK with Fergie, although there was one occasion where I threaded to knock his head off. He accused me of trying to poach Gordon Strachan and of leaking the details to the press. He phoned me up and there were claymores in his voice.

I said, 'You aren't talking to one of your silly players now, Alex. If you don't shut up, I will come over there and personally shut you up.' That night Fergie was driving over to Hull to try to sign Nick Barmby and he rang me from his car. 'I'm sorry, Ron. I've found out who did it and it wasn't you.' He could be gracious in defeat.

It was while I was at Hillsborough that I did some of my best transfer business. I used to see a lot of Dave Bassett, who was managing Sheffield United at the time. 'My wife wants to know why you can buy pricey players and I can't,' he once said to me.

'It's simple, Dave. I buy four players for £500,000 (which was quite a bit of money for the time) while you buy twenty footballers for £100,000. All you do is swap like for like. I try to bring in players who are going to raise the quality of the team.'

I bought Roland Nilsson for £300,000, a phenomenal professional, one of the best I have ever worked with. John Sheridan cost £600,000 from Nottingham Forest, Dalian Atkinson from Ipswich – they could have played in anyone's Premier League team.

Roland's professionalism and ability to turn his hand to almost anything became a byword in the dressing room. When he played tennis he looked like Stefan Edberg, he was dressed immaculately. We began the season at Ipswich and were staying in a hotel out in the Suffolk countryside, where they were staging a wedding. There were marquees and, in the middle of one room, a grand piano.

Phil King, who was the dressing-room village idiot, began bashing it tunelessly as if he were auditioning for a duet with Les Dawson. I ushered him away but later we heard this beautiful piece of classical music coming from the room and there was Roland sitting at the piano.

When I came to the club, Sheffield Wednesday already had a core of decent players like David Hirst, Nigel Worthington and Nigel Pearson. What they all possessed was a fantastic attitude to the game. It reminded me very much of the team I had in my first spell at West Brom. They were all mates, they stuck together. There were one or two scallywags among them – John Sheridan was one – which I don't mind, because characters can add spice.

I bought Shez from Nottingham Forest, where he had played one game, a League Cup tie at Huddersfield. In Brian Clough's regime, first Peter Taylor and then Ronnie Fenton would be in general charge of bringing players in. But there would occasionally be one Cloughie would take against from the very start. Asa Hartford was one and Shez was another.

I talked to Sheridan about coming to Sheffield and John said no, he wanted to prove himself at Forest. I could understand that; he had just arrived from Leeds on the strong recommendation of Jimmy Armfield and, logically, there would be no sense in moving now.

I mentioned it to Brian and back came those nasal tones: 'He's got no fucking chance here,' he said. 'I'll tell you what, ring me at nine-thirty tomorrow morning and he'll be wanting to come.' His first game was against Forest at the City Ground and we won 1–0.

John loved football. If he had been injured or kicked on a Saturday, you'd ask if he wanted to come in for some treatment on the Sunday and he'd always go, 'No, gaffer, I'll be fine, see you on Monday.' I heard that he would go back up to Manchester and play with his brother for a Sunday league pub team. He could be an absolute handful to manage. He had his own vocabulary which included using 'crisp packet' as a term of abuse.

I would put him in the same class as Glenn Hoddle. He could take fabulous free-kicks and had a way of disguising them. We were facing Chelsea in the semi-finals of the League Cup at Stamford Bridge and John had tried three or four times to play a free-kick past the edge of the wall for someone to run on to. It was a tactic Billy Bremner had made his own at Leeds. For this one, Dennis Wise goes on the edge of the wall and shouts, 'Not getting away with it this time, Shez.'

Sheridan played the ball wide to Nigel Worthington, who ran over the ball and played it through for Peter Shirtliff to score and up goes this cry to Dennis Wise: 'Are you sure, you crisp packet?'

In another life, David Hirst could have done stand-up. He had a fantastic array of one-liners and a comedian's sense of timing. He was an old-school footballer from Yorkshire mining stock. Early on in my time with him he made a fabulous, muscular run against Newcastle and then belted it into the top corner of the net at the Gallowgate End of St James' Park. Afterwards, I asked why he'd chosen that moment to shoot because a couple of strides would have seen him in a better position. 'Because I was knackered, gaffer,' came the reply.

On New Year's Day 1990 we played Manchester City at Hillsborough. I took the squad to the Hallam Tower hotel so they would be rested for the match. Breakfast was at eight and when the players came down I had made sure there was a bottle of champagne on every table. 'Happy New Year,' I said. 'Help yourself to a glass.'

Hirsty opened the scoring but then our keeper, Kevin Pressman, got himself injured and had to be taken off. In those days it was very rare to have a substitute goalkeeper on the bench so David volunteered to go in goal.

Much later, he told me why. 'When you offered us all champagne, some, like Roland Nilsson, didn't want any,' he said. 'So I stayed behind and hoovered up the rest of them. When Kevin got injured I said to myself, "I have to go in goal because I can't carry on here."'

Nigel Pearson had a big personality, the best skipper I ever had. When he was in charge at Leicester, he had the reputation of being a dour, humourless man, when in truth he can be very funny. He took part in David Hirst's testimonial at Hillsborough and played on the right wing, where he pulled off a perfect impersonation of Chris Waddle, complete with rolling shoulders and the bandy-legged gait.

The dressing room at Hillsborough had bigger and better players than Nigel but he was always able to keep them in line. That is what made him a decent manager, and he wasn't the only one in that team who went into management.

Roland Nilsson managed Coventry, Malmo and Copenhagen. Nigel Worthington took Norwich into the Premier League, Chris Turner worked at Hartlepool and Sheffield Wednesday, while John Sheridan, the one man I would never have picked out as a manager, had some pretty reasonable success at Chesterfield, Plymouth and Oldham.

Once, on a pre-season training camp, he broke a curfew and I nearly smacked him across the room. We were staying in Acqui Terme in northern Italy. It was an old spa town and it was a bit like staying in Buxton, Derbyshire. We were staying in a rambling old mansion that offered mud baths as a speciality. Suddenly, out of nowhere came this army of beautiful women – Acqui Terme had been chosen to host the preliminary heats of the Miss Italy contest.

It was then that I absolutely insisted on the curfew. Shez was one of three who broke it and he came down the next morning to have it out with me. We had our row and then he walked away up the stairs of the old hall. As he did so, the players called out, 'You did well there, Shez.' As I walked away I could hear Sheridan shout, 'Shut up, you crisp packets.'

I gave him his passport and told him to stay in his room, because missing training would hurt him more than a fine, and I gathered the rest of the boys round. 'I need your opinion lads,' I said. 'Shall I get rid of Sheridan?'

Danny Wilson, a top pro who had just joined Sheffield Wednesday, looked aghast: 'No, gaffer, we need him.' It was the opinion of just about everyone around the table. 'Well,' I said, 'you've made the decision. It's up to you now.' I, of course, had not the slightest intention of sacking John Sheridan but that meeting played its part in getting Sheffield Wednesday both to promotion and to Wembley in the same season. I'd given them some responsibility and a stake in the coming season. They paid me back.

Carlton Palmer was one of my first signings and would count as one of my best. Given that he is associated with some of England's worst displays, particularly the failure to qualify for the 1994 World Cup, that might sound strange, but Carlton was a highly effective footballer, a much, much better player than people remember.

He did what very few midfielders will do now. He ran at people, he ran beyond the ball and beyond the strikers. If you examine modern Premier League strikers – with the exception of Dele Alli at Tottenham – they tend to be happy to sit behind the ball. Carlton was prepared to run and that opened up space for people like John Sheridan.

He missed the League Cup final with injury but he was part of the Sheffield Wednesday side that, under Trevor Francis, made both domestic cup finals. When he and David Hirst went to Southampton in 1997, the club was dead in the water, with four points from nine games, the kind of beginning that did for Aston Villa in the 2015/16 season. Southampton finished twelfth and Carlton played no small part in that.

When England played Holland in Rotterdam in 1993 – the defeat that effectively finished their chances of qualification – Carlton played on the right of midfield in an attempt to stop Frank de Boer getting forward. He did exactly as he was told and England reached half time at 0–0, at which point he was taken off by Graham Taylor.

In the second half, the Dutch broke through twice, which is ironic given that Carlton took so much flak for England's failure to qualify.

He is now the director of football at one of China's most prestigious schools, Wellington College in Shanghai, where fees can be as high as £29,000 a year. Carlton is nobody's fool.

Winning the League Cup and promotion in the same season removed the stain of relegation but there was one wound that was harder to heal. I was, of course, manager of Sheffield Wednesday on 15 April 1989, the afternoon Hillsborough became infamous for reasons other than football. I wasn't at the FA Cup semi-final between Liverpool and Nottingham Forest that ended in the deaths of 96 supporters.

I'd gone to watch Chelsea play Leicester at Filbert Street. The irony was it looked as if there was going to be a serious incident there. Chelsea fans were sat above the Leicester supporters and the atmosphere seemed evil. I was in the directors' box and said, 'This is going to go off here – big time.'

I made to leave and some of the fans sitting in front asked, 'What's wrong, Ron, are you worried about your car?'

'Yes, I am, actually.'

When I got to the car, I turned on the radio and what had happened at Hillsborough began to come through. I rang my office at Hillsborough and got through to my dad. He was there with Lawrie McMenemy and Jack Charlton. He said, 'Something terrible has happened.'

However, it was only when I was home and watching television that I realised quite how terrible it all was. What struck me was that those who were killed – and some were very young because the kids would go the front of the terrace to see better – had done everything they were supposed to. They had mostly turned up an hour before kick-off, as the police wanted, and they had gone to the front of the pen, where they were most vulnerable.

We didn't play at Hillsborough for almost a month and when we did there was a strange, eerie atmosphere around the stadium. There was, for some time afterwards, a strange relic of the disaster. We used to change at Hillsborough before going to training and once I walked into the referee's room and there was a crash barrier from the Leppings Lane End, bent and twisted.

# THIRTEEN

IT WAS THE KIND OF SCENARIO A MANAGER DREAMS OF. AN open-topped bus to board, a trophy to parade, promotion to celebrate with half a city. The problem was that when the parade was over, I would be leaving the bus and leaving Sheffield Wednesday.

If I had a club, a team I supported, it would be Aston Villa. I had been offered the chance to manage them three times before and I thought that if I turned them down once more, the opportunity would never come again.

I didn't move to Sheffield when I joined Wednesday. I would stay at the now derelict Hallam Tower hotel or commute, driving past Villa's training ground at seven in the morning. Whenever I went by Bodymoor Heath, I would think how convenient it would be if I could just turn in and start coaching.

Two days before the grand parade, news of Villa's interest began to leak. Someone had overheard a conversation between my accountant – I didn't employ an agent – and Aston Villa. Soon I was taking a phone call from a Birmingham radio station asking to confirm the story. As a manager, my policy was never to tell a direct lie because it will always rebound on you. So I said, 'It's a funny old game and you never know quite what's going to happen in football.' Or something like that.

When I reached Sheffield, there were fans waiting, asking to know what was going on. The chairman, Dave Richards, took me to one side. 'You can't leave,' he said. 'If you stay, you can have a Rolls-Royce and a driver.'

'I can just imagine me turning up at Hartlepool in a chauffeur-driven Rolls-Royce, Dave. The locals will be so impressed.'

What impressed me more was Cliff Woodward, a Sheffield Wednesday director I really liked, telling me he would resign if I quit. The pressure that day in South Yorkshire grew so intense that I more or less agreed to stay. I phoned my wife, Maggie, and said, 'We're staying in Rome.' We used to call Sheffield that because they were both built on seven hills.

The lads have told me that when I boarded the bus for the parade they knew I was leaving, but I wasn't so sure. On the Monday, Steve Stride, the Aston Villa secretary, called my home and spoke to Maggie, a conversation I wasn't aware of until two years later.

'What would it take to get Ron to the Villa?'

'Why don't you double your offer,' said Maggie.

Steve Stride was one of the very best people I ever worked with. He was straight, he was very good at his job and, perhaps most importantly, he was an Aston Villa fan. When you talked to him, you got a sense of how the supporters were thinking, which was good for the chairman Doug Ellis and for me. He wasn't a dominant character but if he told you, 'I am afraid you can't do that,' you'd listen instead of replying, 'Who says I can't?'

Out of nowhere, he called to offer me vastly improved terms.

I decided I would go and rang Richards. 'I'm sorry, Dave, I am telling you now that I have got to do it. I am resigning. I'll tell you something else, you also have twenty-four hours to sort Nigel Pearson's contract out.' Nigel's contract at Sheffield Wednesday was coming to an end and the club had messed him around as to whether it would be renewed. I had already told Nigel that, if he couldn't get the deal settled, I would sort him with a contract at Aston Villa. If I were being really ruthless, I would have simply taken him with me.

I'd known Dr Jo Venglos, the man I was due to replace, and liked him a lot. When I was at Manchester United, my father used to send his son football memorabilia. One of my first television gigs was the 1980 European Championship in Italy. Venglos was managing the reigning champions, Czechoslovakia, who this time finished third.

Then, before security became absolutely rigid, you would walk into a team's training camp, walk over and watch them practise. One day I might go over to see the West Germans, the next the Czechs. I was introduced to Jo and enjoyed talking football with him.

In April 1991, he was in charge of an Aston Villa side that was thrashed 5–1 at home by Manchester City. David White scored four and the headline in the next day's *Birmingham Mail* was: 'For God's Sake, Go Dr Jo', which I thought was scandalous.

A few days later we played Villa in a reserve game at Hillsborough and I talked to him about the situation at Villa Park. He told me he was going to resign. I said, 'Whatever you do, don't walk out. Make sure they pay up your contract.'

I gave the advice without thinking I'd the beneficiary but they did settle his contract and then the tide of events began pulling me towards Aston Villa.

If I was leaving Sheffield Wednesday, I told myself I would be leaving it in a much better state than I found it. I recommended to Dave Richards that he appoint Trevor Francis as my replacement. The squad was set, he would not have to change very much and he knew the players.

For my number two at Aston Villa, I chose Andy Gray. He had been working for BSkyB who, before they landed the contract for the Premier League, had a very thin roster of games to cover. Andy commentated on Scottish football, which was one of the few leagues they did have the rights to, and he would go to games while he was my assistant.

However, because they had so little football, Sky kept reshowing the games, which made Doug Ellis wonder how much time Andy was actually spending at the club. Doug imagined he must be going off to commentate on four or five games a week.

While I was away covering the 1992 European Championships in Sweden, Doug called Andy in and basically gave him a choice of going to Sky or staying on at Aston Villa. By that time, however, Andy knew Sky would land the contract to cover the Premier League and that he would have a big role in their coverage. His bread was more thickly buttered on the other side.

Andy would have made a fine manager. He knew the game well and had a good presence about him. Like a lot of footballers coming straight into management, the one thing he might have found hard was that you can't do 'players' hours' as a manager. He thought that once you'd done your morning session and had your lunch that was it for the day. As a manager, you had to be the first professional at the ground and the last to leave.

At that time, there was a generation of managers – Harry Redknapp, myself, Barry Fry, Fergie, Jim Smith – who would spend their weekday nights pounding the motorway system to watch matches where a footballer might spark your interest.

The game, with its emphasis on 'world footballers', has changed. When Ken Bates appointed Ruud Gullit to manage Chelsea, he remarked that 'you couldn't expect Ruud to go up to Peterborough on a Tuesday night to watch a player'.

One of the last Premier League managers to spend a lot of time watching smaller clubs in action was David Moyes at Everton. He signed Tim Cahill from Millwall, Phil Jagielka from Sheffield United, Joleon Lescott from Wolves, Leighton Baines from Wigan, John Stones from Barnsley and Seamus Coleman from Sligo Rovers. He went and he watched them.

You look at the success Leicester have had with Jamie Vardy, who played at Stocksbridge Park Steels, Halifax and Fleetwood Town, and you wonder how many other nuggets are being left undiscovered?

The problem Premier League clubs have is the absence of a reserve league, like the old Central League. Liverpool had a superb scout in Geoff Twentyman, who signed Kevin Keegan and Ray Clemence from

Scunthorpe and Ian Rush from Chester.

He signed them specifically for Liverpool reserves and it was there that they would be judged and given time to prove themselves. That structure doesn't exist any more. There is an Under-21 league but it would be difficult to make a signing and give the player twelve months to prove himself in an Under-21 league that is not nearly as competitive as the old Central League used to be.

The endless motorway has now been replaced by an endless stream of player statistics that form the theory of Moneyball – the use of statistics to identify potential transfers. The club that has suffered more in the pursuit of Moneyball than any other in recent times has been Aston Villa.

They had a chief executive in Tom Fox, who was not a football man, a sporting director in Hendrik Almstadt, a man Arsene Wenger thought should be let nowhere near the Villa training ground, and Paddy Riley, a director of scouting and recruitment who relied extensively on computers and statistics. They were precisely the sort of people who had they appeared on *Only Fools and Horses* would have been fleeced of everything. Their Bundesliga specialist lived in Australia.

The gut feeling that a football man has when watching someone at close quarters was almost completely dispensed with. The only time I have spent significant money for any player without seeing him in the flesh was when I paid £750,000 to Gothenburg to bring Niclas Alexandersson to Sheffield Wednesday and then it was on the recommendation of someone I trusted implicitly – Mick Brown who had been my assistant at Old Trafford and was now Manchester United's chief scout. Alexandersson became Wednesday's player of the season in 2000 and was sold to Everton for £2.5m.

One of my first signings at Kettering was Joe Kiernan, a left-sided midfielder who was with Northampton as they went through the divisions to reach the top flight in 1965. I spoke to someone who had worked with him who said, 'Be careful, he is a barrack-room lawyer.' I found him totally committed to the cause.

When I was at West Bromwich Albion, I had seen Peter Withe a lot and was very interested in bringing him to the Hawthorns until someone told me, 'When the going gets tough, he doesn't.' I had watched Withe at Nottingham Forest diving headfirst into the mud in the penalty area, nearly getting his head kicked in. He looked tough enough to me but I didn't pursue the move as hard as I should have and had I not had that piece of 'advice' I might have sealed the transfer. Sometimes you can ask too many people.

Stats have a role but only once you have identified the player – it can't be the other way around. When Manchester United identified Bastian Schweinsteiger, one statistic that should have alarmed them was that in each of his last three seasons with Bayern Munich, he had played fewer games than in the last one. That dwindling pattern continued at Old Trafford.

Judged by the standards of Aston Villa under Tom Fox and Randy Lerner, Doug Ellis seems a hugely impressive figure. I remember first coming across him at the Royal Lancaster Hotel in London. I had ordered a bottle of champagne and Doug came over to me and said, 'If I were your chairman, I wouldn't allow you to do that.'

'That's why you're not my chairman,' I replied. But, after several false starts, that is precisely what he became.

He had first offered me the Villa job when I was at Manchester United. We had gone to a mutual friend's house and talked it through but I concluded that I couldn't walk out on Manchester United. It cropped up again after Aston Villa's relegation in 1987, but they appointed Graham Taylor and when Graham left three years later to manage England, he offered to recommend me to the board.

But I had just been relegated with Sheffield Wednesday and had delivered a speech urging the team to stick together. It would have been particularly crass to have walked out a few days after giving it. In 1991, the club was in much better shape than it had been for years and I felt I could leave with my head high.

If you want to see Doug Ellis's monument, go to Villa Park and look around you. He was responsible for the transformation of the ground into one of the most imposing in England. He did the same for the training ground at Bodymoor Heath.

You could not be a weak manager with him. If you wanted a player, he would back you. You would have to make out your case and you'd have to make it out well but, if you did, you would get the money. Some of his managers criticised him publicly and I thought that was wrong. I had my arguments with Doug Ellis but I would have them to his face.

He was at his core a lonely man. Doug had a lot of hangers-on but I don't think he had a genuine friend in the world. When he sacked me in November 1994 he said I had spent too much time at the training ground. What he really wanted me to do was to come over and let him talk about his boat, which was moored in Majorca.

At Christmas Eve 1993, we were in the unusual position of not having another game for five days so I told the players I would work them hard, give them a blast on the banjo and they could have Christmas Day off. We weren't due to play our next game, at Norwich, until the 29 December.

I had a party to go to at Gary Newbon's house. I was the last one at the ground, Maggie was at the hairdressers, I was making a few phone calls in the office. It must have been about two-thirty. Doug knocked on the door. His wife had gone to Majorca and he was on his own.

'Hello, Ron. I thought we'd do what we do every Christmas and take you and the staff out for a few drinks and then have some fish and chips.'

This was my third Christmas at Aston Villa and I had never come across this tradition before. 'I can't Doug, I'm going to Gary Newbon's party.'

'Gary's having a party?'

'Oh yes, they'll all be there, Jasper Carrott, Jeff Farmer (who was the head of ITV Sport), all the boys will be there.' Then, I decided to scatter a bit of mischief into the conversation. 'It's a safe bet you've been invited and Marion (his genuinely wonderful secretary) has forgotten to tell you. You live near Jeff Farmer, why don't you ask him to take you.'

The party was going with a swing and we'd been there a couple of hours and in walks Jeff Farmer, a man who was never very good at hiding his feelings. His face was thunderous. Behind him was Doug.

He came out on my first pre-season, which was in Germany, ostensibly to meet the new players. When he appeared at our training camp he put a Villa tracksuit on and stood at the sidelines with the coach driver watching us practise free-kicks.

I yelled over, 'We're short in the wall. Will you two come over and get in the wall.' They did and Gordon Cowans, who was about to take the kick, went over to me and said, 'What you do want me to do now that the chairman's in the wall?'

'Put your foot back and hit it at him as hard as you can.' The ball fizzed past Doug's face.

One of Doug's conceits was that he invented the bicycle kick. It is a story Andy Gray is fond of telling and takes place when Doug was playing for the army in Italy alongside Stanley Matthews, Tommy Finney and Tommy Lawton. As Doug relates the story, the crowd invariably grows from a few hundred to a stadium crammed with tens of thousands of screaming Italians.

The punchline is that as a cross comes over Doug says, 'I realised Frank – Swift, that is – wasn't going to get it so I turned and swivelled and hooked the ball over my shoulder. As one the crowd rose and chanted: "*La Bicicletta!*"' I'd heard it for the first time on that pre-season tour. Andy had just finished relating it when Shaun Teale came over and said, 'Gaffer, the chairman's just told us how he invented the bicycle kick.'

We had the first week's training at Aston University because Bodymoor Heath was being refurbished. I told the staff, 'Let's go and have an eight-a-side against the kids,' because that is how you got to know them.

The first team were not due back for another week and in the staff team were the likes of me, Richard Money, Peter Withe, physio Jim Walker and Andy Gray – and Tony Cascarino, who was then Aston Villa's record signing but had come back early to work on his fitness.

I had seen Tony play for Millwall and Ireland and he wasn't my type of player but I thought I'd give him a chance. That day he played abysmally. Every ball seemed to bounce off his shins and as we were walking up the hill back to the changing rooms, I said to Andy Gray, 'Cass has got to go before anyone sees him play.'

At the same time, Cass had gone into the pavilion, thrown his boots down in front of Jim Walker and said, 'I don't think I've done myself any favours.' Villa had paid £1.1m for Cascarino but the best offer we had was £750,000 from Wimbledon until Liam Brady, who was managing Celtic, offered us the chance to get our money back.

If I could, I would have brought the entire Sheffield Wednesday team with me to Villa Park, but I did know that, at Liverpool, Graeme Souness had a left-back surplus to requirements. He had three, Steve Staunton, David Burrows and Gary Ablett. Of those, Steve was probably the best of the lot but Liverpool were back in Europe for the first time since the Heysel disaster and UEFA rules then restricted the number of foreigners you could field. Steve was born in Drogheda and for that reason Souness was inclined to let him go for £1.1m.

David Platt had spent the close season determined to force a transfer through to Bari and it was obvious from the first session that his heart was not at Aston Villa. I said to Andy Gray, 'We have a problem and we don't want the problem manifesting itself and infecting other people, so let's get rid of it now.' Bari agreed a fee of £5.5m, which was then a British transfer record. I was determined to rebuild the team as quickly as I could, which involved commuting from Birmingham to Hamburg, where the team was based for pre-season, and then back again. When I signed Paul Mortimer from Charlton I gave him my car keys and told him to drive me straight to the airport.

Andy, who had played with him at Everton, recommended we sign Kevin Richardson, who was at Real Sociedad with Dalian Atkinson. We signed them both and I had toyed with the idea of making it three by including John Aldridge, who was also at Sociedad, in the deal. He was then 32 and I thought there wouldn't be a lot left in his career. That, as it turned out, was a mistake. He left Spain for Tranmere Rovers where he played for another seven, highly-successful years.

We bought Shaun Teale from Bournemouth and Dariusz Kubicki, a decent full-back who had captained Poland, from Legia Warsaw. I also signed Cyrille Regis, whom I'd wanted to work with again ever since I left West Brom. He was at Coventry and they thought he was finished but every time I'd watched Big Cyrille he seemed to be their best player. For my first game as manager of Aston Villa, I had eight players making their debuts, and after half an hour of that match you would have thought I'd picked six of them up on the motorway coming to the game.

To my disbelief, that game was away to Sheffield Wednesday. Doug insisted on coming on the coach with us and as we approached Hillsborough he moved away, joking he didn't want to be hit by a stray sniper's bullet. There were a few 'Judas' chants but that kind of thing has never bothered me. These days, however, there seems to be a lot more vitriol added to the chants.

After ten minutes Villa were two down and the way it was going we were going to be ten down by half-time. Just before the interval, we won a corner. Chris Woods was making his debut in goal for Sheffield Wednesday and Andy Gray, who had watched a lot of Scottish football for BSkyB, turned to me and said, 'He had a bad injury at Rangers and he's not as brave as he used to be.'

The corner is delivered, Big Cyrille goes in and clashes with the keeper, the ball goes out for another corner. The corner goes in again, Cyrille is there but Chris Woods isn't and the deficit is 2–1. In the dressing room at Hillsborough, I told the lads, 'You'll win this now because they won't know whether to stick or twist – whether to hold on for two-one or hit us for six.

In the second half Dalian equalised and then from their corner we broke away and Steve Staunton, from left-back, found himself clean through to strike the winner. A mate of mine, a Sheffield man, turned to me and said, 'Who writes your scripts?'

# FOURTEEN

I WAS AT THE BIGGEST CLUB IN ENGLAND'S SECOND CITY
just as the idea of a Premier League was being floated. I must admit I
had no idea that this would the moment when the English game would
transform itself to the extent that, financially at least, it would overshadow the rest of Europe. I saw it as a rather pointless name change.

It produced the kind of vocabulary I loathed. Fans became 'custom-
ers', the team became 'the group' and the club became 'the brand'.
Commercially, it has been an outstanding success, although from a
playing point of view the season it produced its greatest story – Leicester's
charge to the title – the standard of football was perhaps the weakest
it has ever been.

Usually, the only thing I bet on is golf but when the odds were released
for the Premier League's opening season in 1992, Aston Villa were 50–1.
My first season in charge had seen us finish seventh, four places behind
Sheffield Wednesday, but I could sense the squad was starting to gel and,
at those prices, I thought it worth a punt and so did Paul McGrath. As
the season climaxed and it became a race between Villa, Manchester
United and Norwich, we became a little nervous and got our physio, Jim
Walker, to lay the bets off.

We had Dalian Atkinson up front alongside Cyrille Regis. Cyrille was 33 when I began working with him again and, while he'd done a very impressive job in my first season, he was becoming prone to muscle problems.

I tried Frank McAvennie, who the lads were very impressed with because he was dating a Page Three girl but who, however hard he worked, wasn't going to make the grade. We went unsuccessfully for Hans Gillhaus, a Dutch striker at Aberdeen.

The forward I had long been interested in was Dean Saunders. I had tried to buy him when he was at Derby but he chose to go to Liverpool, although after only one season at Anfield, I heard Graeme Souness was prepared to let him go.

We agreed a fee for £2.5m very quickly but Doug Ellis dragged his heels as he attempted to chip away at the price. Doug was trying to outsmart the Liverpool secretary, Peter Robinson, who had worked with Bill Shankly, Bob Paisley and Kenny Dalglish. It was a pointless waste of our time.

The impasse lasted for two weeks, with Deano ringing me up asking when the move was going to happen or if it was going to happen. I was starting to become anxious because my rule of thumb was that my most successful transfers had been those done quickly. The ones that had taken an age were generally those that had not come off.

Things were not going well on the pitch. Aston Villa had won only one of our first five Premier League games. We had just lost 3-1 at home to Chelsea and the chairman was starting to take a lot of flak on the radio phone-ins. On the Saturday I was driving to Villa Park for our fixture against Crystal Palace when Steve Stride rang me with a query: 'The chairman wants to know the state of play with the Saunders deal.'

'Steve, the deal is exactly what it was two weeks ago.'

'OK, we will do it.'

Before kick-off I went to the PA announcer and asked for his microphone and marched towards the Holte End. 'I want you behind us, today,' I said. 'I am telling you now, the deal is done. He is coming.'

As I walked off, I thought I would look an absolute idiot if everything fell through, but we beat Crystal Palace 3–0 – and we were completely useless. It was one of those victories where the crowd plays a critical part. They kept with us all afternoon.

Dean signed that week and made his debut in a 1–1 draw at the champions, Leeds. His first home game was against Liverpool. He scored twice and Liverpool's Ronnie Rosenthal managed to take the ball past our keeper, Nigel Spink, only to hit the crossbar in front of a completely empty net. We won 4–2 and it was a catalyst for everything that followed. We lost one of our next twelve games and in Dalian Atkinson and Dean Saunders we had the best strike partnership in the Premier League. They were unstoppable.

I first saw Dalian when I was at West Brom for the second time and he was playing for Ipswich, and I scouted him when they played Queens Park Rangers. I liked the look of him and of Les Ferdinand who was playing for QPR. He was then named in an Ipswich reserve team that was due to play at Swindon. I watched him again and then called his manager, John Duncan.

'Look, I will offer you £25,000 for him and I could probably stretch to a bit more.'

'Ron, I'd love to but I can't do business now because it's Thursday and I'll need Dalian in the squad for the weekend.'

Dalian scored twice, massively increasing his value, so I thought I would wait, let the fuss die down, before calling John Duncan again. The response was the same: I'd called late in the week, they had a big game against Middlesbrough, whose central defensive pairing of Gary Pallister and Tony Mowbray was formidable, and they wanted to play Dalian at the weekend. Ipswich won 4–0 at Portman Road and Dalian's contribution was a hat-trick. I called John Duncan on the Monday and began the conversation with the words: 'This might be the most futile question ever but . . .' The answer was no.

A year later, in 1989, I managed to sign Dalian for Sheffield Wednesday for £450,000. Towards the end of his time at Aston Villa, he was taunted by the fans with the nickname 'Sicknote' because of his injury record but he didn't miss a game at Hillsborough and, when Wednesday were relegated, Real Sociedad paid £1.6m for him.

The problem he encountered in La Liga was that he would shine on the big stage. At the Bernabeu or the Nou Camp he would be inspired. Against the likes of Gijon or Oviedo he would disappear, and these were the clubs Sociedad needed to beat. It was the same at Aston Villa. He was a certain pick for Old Trafford but not if you got Exeter in the cup.

His partnership with Saunders was at its best when we played Wimbledon at Selhurst Park. Villa won 3–2: Deano scored twice, while Dalian's goal was astonishing. He took the ball from inside his own half, rode three tackles and then, with Dean Saunders screaming for the ball, he saw Hans Segers off his line and chipped him wonderfully. It was belting down with rain and as he ran over to the Villa fans, one of them brought an umbrella out for him.

Because it was at Wimbledon the stand behind Segers was empty terracing, which lessened the impact of the strike. Had it been scored at Old Trafford, Highbury or Anfield, the coverage would have been phenomenal. It was still voted Goal of the Season by *Match of the Day* and is up there with the best goals ever scored by a team I managed.

Cyrille Regis's goal for West Brom at Manchester City would have been a serious rival. Gary Owen played with Cyrille for four years at The Hawthorns but he never gave him a better pass than when he was playing for City. Cyrille intercepted it, went past Dave Watson, past Mike Doyle, past Paul Power as he moved across him, and then as Joe Corrigan came out of his goal, he slammed it in.

The whole of Maine Road rose to applaud that goal, including Joe Mercer, who was then a director at Manchester City. Our chairman, Bert Millichip, turned to Joe and said, 'But he doesn't score ones like that every week.' That was his chairman's reaction to a once-in-a-lifetime goal.

In December, we played Sheffield Wednesday at Hillsborough and beat them 2–1 with two hammer strikes from Dalian. We were now in third place, eight points behind Norwich, who were the only team that had beaten us since Deano and Dalian were paired up. A couple of days later,

Dalian tore his hamstring in training and that was our first real stumble.

Manchester United were a better side than us but we had a good team, who took four points off United in the season they won the championship for the first time since the days of Best, Law and Charlton.

At the time Mark Bosnich was in phenomenal form, probably the best keeper in the league. The following season we went to Roker Park to play Sunderland in the League Cup. We won 4–1, which sounds a straightforward enough evening, but the scoreline disguises the fact that, but for Mark, Sunderland would have murdered us.

They had a young winger called Martin Smith. Our right-back was Earl Barrett and nobody, not even Ryan Giggs, ran past him, but this boy did. On the bench we looked at each other and thought, 'Where did this lad come from?' There and then I offered Sunderland's manager, Mick Buxton, £1m for Smith. But he suffered a bad injury and the deal faded away.

If Dalian's injury was one turning point, the season swung on Manchester United's desperately late goals to beat Sheffield Wednesday that ended with Alex Ferguson leaping into Brian Kidd's arms on the pitch. It was 10 April 1993, Easter Saturday, and Aston Villa were top of the Premier League. We had just drawn 0–0 at home to Coventry in an absolutely terrible game and, as we walked off, I heard shouts of 'They're getting beat.' That meant that we were still two points clear.

The dressing rooms at Villa Park were then at the top of a flight of stairs and by the time we'd got the top, which must have been five minutes after the final whistle, there was a groan and someone said, 'They've equalised.'

I looked at my watch and it was five to five. 'It will be one of those games,' I said. 'United will play until they win.' Just before the end of normal time, Carlton Palmer, who was in midfield for Sheffield Wednesday, went over to the linesman and asked how much stoppage time there would be. He was told two minutes. He remarked to me ruefully afterwards, 'Six minutes later we were still playing.' As Trevor Francis said, 'They scored in the second leg.'

Although Manchester United were a better side than Aston Villa, my belief had always been that the astonishing pressure to win the title would drag them down. Now, as their late victory over Sheffield Wednesday took them top with five games to go, I wasn't so sure.

We went to Blackburn and in the opening fifteen minutes we absolutely buried them, but didn't take our chances; Blackburn did and we lost 3–0. That was the match that cost us the championship. By the time we played Oldham – the result that guaranteed Manchester United their first title in 26 years – we were looking at snookers.

Football was changing, the old order was going. I never wavered in my belief that for what he achieved and where he achieved it, Brian Clough was the finest manager I have known. But he was struggling with alcohol and his mind didn't seem as sharp and focused as it once was. That month Nottingham Forest would be relegated.

Liverpool, suddenly, were no longer a force. They finished sixth, 25 points off the pace, and even at the start of the season Liverpool hadn't been one of the teams I thought of as serious contenders. Jack Walker was pumping huge amounts of his steel fortune into Blackburn but Alex Ferguson's Manchester United were now the team to beat.

Alex Ferguson built several Manchester United sides but, if you were to pin him down and ask for his favourite, I think Fergie would nominate the 1993/94 Double winning squad. There was power all through the side and there were some strong people in that dressing room: Peter Schmeichel, Mark Hughes, Steve Bruce, Paul Ince, Eric Cantona, Gary Pallister, Roy Keane and Ryan Giggs. The only thing they didn't have was blistering pace through the middle. We faced them in the League Cup final.

In contrast to our first season in the Premier League, Aston Villa were not playing well, and after the semi-final against Tranmere we had gone completely off the boil. The two games against Tranmere were arguably the most eventful I have been involved in.

In the first leg at Prenton Park we were 3–0 down until the last kick of the game, when Dalian Atkinson scored, and as we walked off you would have thought Aston Villa had won. Tranmere's dressing room was very quiet and they seemed deflated by the late goal which, given they had beaten us by two clear goals, seemed strange. If you had told Tranmere's manager, John King, the score before kick-off he and his team would have been elated.

The second leg saw us two up very quickly and then, when John Aldridge ran through, Mark Bosnich cleaned him out. For one very long minute it seemed that Bosnich might be sent off. He wasn't, but Aldridge scored from the penalty to make it 4–3 on aggregate.

We spent the rest of the match battering away at them until a couple of minutes from time, when Dalian scored with a header to level it up. However, with the last kick of normal time, Tranmere were awarded a free-kick; when Liam O'Brien, who I had signed at Manchester United, took it, the ball struck one post, rolled along the line, and hit the other one.

It went to first extra time and then penalties. Ugo Ehiogu had the chance to win the match and struck the bar. Aldridge scored his penalty to take it to sudden death and, with the first of those, Kevin Richardson missed to give O'Brien, who might have won the match in normal time, the chance to take Tranmere to Wembley – but Bosnich saved his penalty. Tony Daley scored his and Bosnich made his third save of the shoot-out to send us through. As a match, it had everything, and even those who had watched Villa at the 1982 European Cup final have told me that League Cup semi beat it for sheer entertainment.

Seven months later, Aston Villa won another penalty shoot-out, this time against Inter Milan in the UEFA Cup. We had lost the first leg 1–0 at the San Siro to a Dennis Bergkamp penalty, which Ray Houghton's goal cancelled out at Villa Park. It was all decided by a shoot-out which ended, much to Kevin Keegan's delight, at after 11 p.m. Keegan was commentating on the match and less than two days later he would be managing a rested and refreshed Newcastle against the exhausted team that had just endured the mental agonies of deciding a match from twelve yards. When he came into my office afterwards, he was laughing his head off. 'My boys have been in bed for the last two hours.'

In those days, teams playing on a Thursday could and did play on a Saturday. Not surprisingly, Newcastle won, 2–0. That season we lost every game we played after a European fixture.

My theory on penalty shoot-outs is that the goalkeeper should not move before the kick is taken because, invariably, two of the five kicks will be placed somewhere near where he is standing. It is slightly different if it is a regular penalty in a match because the player taking it will be a specialist and the keeper will probably have a fair idea of where he might put it.

But in a shoot-out he will be facing one or possibly two who have never taken a penalty in their lives. In those circumstances, he should stay where he is. If you are taking a penalty in a shoot-out, at least hit it hard. I cannot stand tame spot kicks. The best penalty-taker I ever managed was Tony Brown at West Brom and he would slam them. If you wanted someone to score a penalty for your life, it would be Bomber.

The Manchester United side Aston Villa faced in the 1994 League Cup final were a remarkable team in terrific form. When we met at Wembley they had lost one match in six months and were six points clear at the top of the Premier League. Our performances had been patchy and not to the level I would have wanted.

On the Tuesday before the final, I went to Highbury to watch Arsenal draw 2–2 with United. Eric Cantona was sent off when he shouldn't have been but for me the most interesting aspect was the way Arsenal played. George Graham employed three up front – Alan Smith, Ian Wright and Kevin Campbell – and Arsenal hit long balls up to them that seemed to cause United problems.

As I made my way out of Highbury I thought, 'I wonder'. In December at Old Trafford, I had tried to man-mark Cantona using Earl Barrett, who completely blotted him out of the game. Cantona was restricted to two meaningful touches . . . which produced two goals.

For the final, I thought I would use Graham Fenton, a striker who had been on loan at West Brom and Leicester. He was young, strong and powerful. I would try to match Manchester United's power with some of our own. He would play in midfield alongside Kevin Richardson and Andy Townsend. It meant I had to leave out Ray Houghton and Gary Parker, whose emphasis was on skill.

Tony Daley would go out on to one flank, Dalian Atkinson would be on the other and Dean Saunders would be on his own up front. 'You will work your cobblers off,' I told Saunders. 'If you get tired, I will take you off.' I had no real idea who I was going to put on in his place but that's the speech I gave Deano. I told Dalian and Tony, who had astonishing pace, to make the United full-backs run towards their own goal.

The other tactic I emphasised was to keep our midfield three between Cantona and Mark Hughes. We tried to push Cantona deep and, although he inevitably broke through once or twice, it worked.

The biggest risk was to use Steve Staunton, who'd only just recovered from a hernia operation, at left-back. Usually, against Manchester United, I would have picked Bryan Small, because he had the pace to cope with Andrei Kanchelskis. I just thought Steve's greater ability on the ball might be crucial at Wembley.

Manchester United wore yellow and green squares, Aston Villa had a claret-and-blue pinstripe that I'd recalled them playing in when they beat United in the 1957 FA Cup final. The other thing I remember Villa doing before that FA Cup final was training on the beautiful pitches Cadbury's had at Bournville. We trained on the hockey pitches there, which were faster than the football pitches.

In London, I stuck to the build-up I'd used for the 1991 final. Dinner on the Friday night with the wives before moving the players out to Oakley Court at Windsor with Stan Boardman on the coach to Wembley.

It didn't work quite as well as it had with Sheffield Wednesday. Stan had been quite a good footballer and he had a trick where he could flick it around the back of his legs and send the ball high. When we were in the dressing rooms at Wembley, he did it and wondered if any Villa professional would like to have a go. It caused a few problems because none of them could. When Stan was on *This Is Your Life*, I took a football with me and asked him to do the trick for the cameras.

We won 3–1. Dalian and Deano scored, Mark Hughes got one back for Manchester United and then Kanchelskis was sent off for handling on the line and from the penalty we hit the third. The local paper hailed me a 'master tactician', which I found amusing. 'Always enjoy the good times,' Noel Cantwell, who had captained Manchester United to the 1963 FA Cup, once told me. And that night we did.

# FIFTEEN

COVENTRY WERE FAMOUS AS THE CLUB THAT ALWAYS MAN-
aged to avoid relegation. It was a reputation Southampton also had and
which Sunderland have inherited in the last few seasons.

When I was at Coventry we used to joke that if the *Titanic* had been
painted sky-blue it wouldn't have gone down. Every season, however,
used to be the one when it seemed Coventry's luck would not hold and
in February 1995 it seemed this would be the season. Especially as the
Premier League had decreed that four clubs would be relegated to reduce
the size of the division from 22 to 20 teams.

I was approached by the chairman and vice-chairman of Coventry
about becoming their manager. However, they wanted me to groom
a young manager as my assistant who would take over from me in a
couple of years.

I had three people in mind: Ray Wilkins, Chris Waddle and Gordon
Strachan. Of the three Gordon was probably third in line because he
was still playing for Leeds. But, shortly afterwards, in the wake of a poor
performance against Liverpool, Howard Wilkinson persuaded him to
end his playing career at 37 – prematurely as it turned out – and prepare
for management. That is when I called him.

Gordon was involved in the five-a-side games on our training ground at Ryton and I watched him and thought, 'You are still miles better than anything we have got here.'

He agreed to play and was instrumental in Coventry staying up. We had to go to Tottenham for the penultimate game of the season and to survive we had to win. I said to him, 'Gordon, I really need you to play.' He just nodded his head and said, 'OK.'

He destroyed Justin Edinburgh that night. Tormented him. If you asked Justin Edinburgh who his hardest opponent was during his time in the Tottenham defence, he would say 'Gordon Strachan' without thinking. Peter Ndlovu on the other flank did the same to Sol Campbell and Coventry won, 3–1.

I involved Gordon regularly. If a transfer was up for discussion, I would take him to the board meeting at Highfield Road and, even if he didn't say a word, he would get a flavour of how the club operated.

When I was appointed, Coventry also said they couldn't offer the kind of money I'd been on at Aston Villa but they would incentivise it by paying me a pound per person over the average gate at Highfield Road, which was then about 14,000.

We began well. I was manager of the month for March 1995, I brought two or three new players in and publicised the club as much as I could. The attendances reached as much as 23,000. Before a game, Gordon would be studying the tactics, wondering if the opposition were going to have one or two up front, and I'd be studying the stands saying, 'Look, Gordon, there are half a dozen empty seats up there.'

I had been out of work for three months. Doug sacked me in November 1994, a few days after telling the BBC that I was one of the three best managers in the country. Like my dismissal at Manchester United, I hadn't seen it coming.

Aston Villa were in trouble, we had taken one point from nine games and, after beating Inter Milan, we had managed to get ourselves knocked out of the UEFA Cup by Trabzonspor. We were in the bottom four now but there was no panic, no clamour for my dismissal from the Holte End. When my sacking was announced, there was a campaign by the local radio station in Birmingham to have me reinstated.

Doug did it in a fit of pique – the meeting to dismiss me lasted precisely four minutes. Years later, I said to him, 'You lost your temper, didn't you, Doug?'

'I'm afraid I did, Ron.'

Coventry's main attraction was that it was not far from where I lived. There were not many others and one of the problems was that they already had a manager, Phil Neal, when I was approached. I had known Phil since I'd tried to sign him when I was at Kettering and I'd worked with him when he was manager of Bolton. After Mick Brown and I had been sacked at Manchester United, Mick got himself fixed up with Bolton as Phil's number two. But in the summer of 1987, just before he was due to start work, Mick had an accident with a lawnmower which tore off a chunk of his foot.

Mick was a very conscientious man and I knew it would be tormenting him that he couldn't work so I rang up Phil and said, 'Browny is struggling. He wants to try to hobble in but he can't. If you like, I will come in and do his job for you, without being paid, until he is ready to come back to work.'

I'd been doing it a few weeks and was enjoying it when the Bolton chairman, Barry Chaytow, approached me, asking whether I'd like to manage the club. I told him that wasn't why I was there. It was the same thing now. If I became Coventry's manager, it would be awkward.

I said to the Coventry chairman Bryan Richardson, 'Give Phil a bit more time and see what happens.' They had just been knocked out of the FA Cup by Norwich in a replay but on the Saturday they had beaten Crystal Palace and were now out of the relegation zone.

I was in the car going to commentate on a televised game on the Sunday when I got another call from Coventry. I expected the conversation to be along the lines of 'We are going to stick with Phil Neal.'

Instead, it was: 'We have made a decision and he's going.'

'Well, if I go in, could you make sure he is paid up?'

I had been manager of Coventry for two weeks when I got a call from Francis Lee, who was then chairman of Manchester City. He was also very good friends with Bryan Richardson. They would play golf together in Barbados. Franny was offering me the Manchester City job to succeed Brian Horton. 'I can't possibly do it, I've only been here about a fortnight,' I said. 'And anyway, what about your mate, Bryan Richardson? I've got to stay at Coventry.'

'That,' Franny replied, 'is like Sinatra playing Wigan Pier.'

Coventry had a mixture of some very good and some very ordinary players. Dion Dublin and Peter Ndlovu were exceptional but they had very little support. Dion's best position was as a centre-half but he had an astonishing knack of being able to score when he was pushed up and that's where he stayed.

I tried to strengthen by bringing in Noel Whelan from Leeds, who I could not believe were prepared to let him go. Whelan was one of those footballers who if things had gone a bit differently would have played regularly for England.

Carlton Palmer, who was at Elland Road with him, told me that Noel was one the very few footballers who could outrun him. Whelan's problem was that Gordon Strachan had also played in midfield with him at Leeds and wanted to play him there when he took over from me.

I would have played him further forward. There was a bit of Alan Shearer in Noel Whelan. He was not as good in the air but he possessed terrific skill. For Gordon he was a midfielder who would run fifty yards with the ball and pass it ten. On New Year's Day 1996, with banks of snow around the advertising hoardings, we were losing 1–0 at home to Southampton when Noel took the ball on the left flank, cut inside and took it past three defenders before stabbing the ball home. In the 88th minute, the referee, Keith Cooper, blew for full time.

We walked off and, when he realised his error, we came back for another one minute and 35 seconds. In those days, the referees would come into your office for a drink and we gave him as much stick as we could muster over whether he had got a new watch for Christmas.

I have never criticised referees. The only time I came close was when

West Brom were playing Red Star Belgrade in the quarter-finals of the UEFA Cup and the referee gave a really dodgy free-kick late on and Dusan Savic, who was a wonderful player, curled it in our top corner. Red Star won the first leg 1–0 and afterwards the English press were demanding to know what I thought of the referee. 'You know me, lads, I never criticise referees, and I'm not going to make an exception for that prat.'

The boardroom at Highfield Road was like an open house. The hospitality flowed and I would get home from Saturday afternoon matches later than I did from European trips with Manchester United and Aston Villa. I kept telling Bryan Richardson that if he closed the hospitality lounges at seven o'clock we could afford to buy a new player.

I was obviously operating at the bottom end of the transfer market but one day Bryan came into my office while we were trying to do a deal for Andy Linighan, who was then at Arsenal, and asked, 'If you could buy any centre-half in the country, who would you have?'

'Well, that would depend who is available, chairman. The most available centre-half would be Chris Coleman at Crystal Palace. But he would cost around three million. I'm trying to do a deal for Andy Linighan for a tenth of that money.'

Richardson told me to make a bid. The club had brought in a new director called Geoffrey Robinson, who was powerful for two reasons. He was the Labour MP for Coventry North West, who was to become Paymaster General in the Blair Government, a job he was to lose after giving Peter Mandelson an undeclared loan to buy a house. He was also a big player in business in the Midlands, who had worked with British Leyland, Triumph and Jaguar. We called him the Money Man. Geoffrey Robinson had begun putting large sums of cash into the club and I believed he wanted to buy players with sell-on clauses to safeguard his investment.

Coleman was interested and came to watch us play. In December 1995 we were at home to the champions, Blackburn. Kenny Dalglish had quit as manager the moment they won the league to become a very distant director of football and Ray Harford was in charge. They had made a dismal showing in the Champions League and they were well off the pace in the Premier League but the fact remained they were champions of England and Coventry City were stone-cold bottom. We beat them 5–0.

Had we won by just the odd goal, Blackburn might not have panicked, but Ray Harford was convinced he needed to reorganise his defence and promptly outbid us for Coleman.

In October 1996, Coventry had just fought out a goalless draw at Highbury in what was Arsene Wenger's first home match as Arsenal manager. In the aftermath of a game, a manager is going here, there and everywhere, talking to the team, sometimes the directors and always the press. I bumped into Ken Jones, a veteran journalist whom I'd known for years, and was talking to him when Geoffrey Robinson came across and said, 'Ron, can I have a word?'

I told him to hold on until I had finished talking to Ken and the moment I said it, I sensed I had rubbed him up badly. He wasn't happy. Two days later, I had a call from another journalist informing me that moves were afoot to have me replaced.

It rumbled on for another couple of weeks. We were due to play Everton on a Monday night in early November and just before the game it was put to me by the chairman, Bryan Richardson, that I should step down and become director of football while Gordon took over the running of the first team.

'Before we go on,' I told Bryan, 'we need some guidelines about who is responsible for what and which of us in charge. If Gordon is in charge of everything, the first thing I am going to do is ask him for a rise.'

Bryan walked out of the room with a parting shot that we should 'sort it out between yourselves', which struck me as a total lack of leadership.

I am a firm believer in the fact that the role of director of football, if done properly, can be a real benefit to a club. The director of football should be the man who appoints the manager so the manager knows that if he runs into any problems the director of football is in his camp.

Ten years later, Sky made a film called Big Ron Manager, which had me going in to trouble-shoot at clubs that were in a bit of difficulty. When I went to Peterborough, the first thing I said to the manager, Steve Bleasdale, was, 'Don't be looking over your shoulder. I don't want your job and, if I did, Barry Fry (we call Barry Fry Peterborough's chairman. He wasn't actually. He was the owner.) wouldn't give it to me now. Any help I can give you, I will give, and I won't say anything to anybody that I wouldn't say to your face.'

As a manager, I was never afraid of people with knowledge. Even at Cambridge, I used to go to the big international matches just on the off chance I would bump into someone I could corner for a bit of advice. When Bill Nicholson used to come to the Abbey Stadium, I would make sure I talked to him. Stan Cullis was always willing to give you advice and would often write you letters.

That's why I would phone Bill Shankly, and when John Docherty and I had come off the phone to him, we felt we could take on the world. When I appointed Dave Sexton at Aston Villa, it was because I wanted his experience, not because I was afraid he might take my job.

The director of football should be there to give advice to the manager about a player he is interested in and what the mood of the boardroom is. The final decision should always rest with the manager but the director of football will often have useful knowledge he can pass on.

I have talked to Alex McLeish about his time at Aston Villa, which was poisoned by the fact he had come to the club from Birmingham City. If I had come in with him in some sort of capacity, I think I could have got the crowd behind him at the start. Perhaps I should have called him.

The pressure at the bottom is constant. Coventry were a team that was always fighting for its life and in March 1996 we lost 1–0 to Southampton in a televised match at the Dell. Jason Dodd, who scored fewer than ten goals in more than 400 league games, found the net with a glancing header and Coventry then battered them to the extent that their keeper, Dave Beasant, was made man of the match by Sky. The result meant that Southampton climbed out of the relegation zone while we fell into it.

Afterwards, I was asked by Sky to do an interview with Richard Keys, who was in the studio. Richard is a passionate Coventry fan, he was born in the city. Normally, I wouldn't do an interview until I had been in the dressing room, but Geoff Shreeves told me they needed some footage for Richard and Andy Gray in the studio, so I put on the headphones they used and heard Richard say that if Coventry were going to escape relegation, 'you need to show more than you did tonight'.

I had known Richard since he was working with Piccadilly Radio when I was managing Manchester United and I was furious. 'I am not going to whip my players whatever your silly (video) machines say. By the way, who was man of the match tonight?'

When Keys said Dave Beasant, I took my headphones off and tossed them to Geoff Shreeves. People said I threw them at him but I didn't. I went into the dressing room and told the players, 'If you perform like that for the rest of the season, I'll be happy.' Then, I went into the main lounge at the Dell and everybody started clapping.

The 1995/96 season was a hard one for me because my dad was diagnosed as being terminally ill. One morning I was at a hotel in Liverpool preparing for a game at Everton and got a call that things were very serious. I dashed back to the hospital in Birmingham and then back to Merseyside for the match.

After the final day of the season when we had secured Coventry's future for another year with a goalless draw with Leeds, I went back to hospital to see my dad. They had removed his voice box so he could no longer speak and all he could do was to lift his head from the pillow and give me the thumbs-up.

That was not the only trauma to be endured that season. On 8 April, David Busst suffered one of the worst injuries ever sustained by a professional footballer. It was in the first minute against Manchester United at Old Trafford. David slid in at the far post as a corner was flicked on and seemed to collide with either Denis Irwin or Brian McClair. Even to this day, I am not quite sure what happened. He may not have collided with anyone, simply wrenched his studs into the ground.

The results, though, were horrific. It was a double compound fracture, there was blood everywhere. Peter Schmeichel was physically sick and the game had to be held up for nine minutes.

By the end of the season, it was obvious David would not play again. He was told that if that had happened to him twenty years before, his leg could have been amputated. In only one respect was he fortunate.

Because it had happened at Old Trafford, I was able to contact Fergie and ask if he could send a Manchester United side down to play a testimonial for Bussty, which they did. It was Eric Cantona's final game of football for United and there were 26,000 at Highfield Road. Had David sustained that hideous injury at Wimbledon, there would not have been anything like the same response.

Taking over a struggling club meant anything you suggested was likely to be approved because one thing that terrifies any boardroom is relegation. They are not going to interfere with any changes you make to training because the previous sessions won't exactly have been working.

I made mistakes and one of them was signing Gary McAllister. He was too good a player for the situation Coventry found themselves in. Gordon Strachan, who had won the championship with him at Leeds, was pushing hard for the deal. He had the choice of Liverpool or Coventry and I believe that had he gone to Anfield they would have won the league in 1997.

Gary could have played in any team I ever managed but he wasn't what a Coventry side struggling to survive required. Having turned Liverpool down, he was on massive wages and, to compound the mistake, I made him captain in place of Dion Dublin.

There were good arguments for it – he had captained Leeds and Scotland – but reports of the money he was on had caused resentment and now a popular guy like Dion had lost the captaincy. Gary was a great professional, who was the polar opposite of Billy Big-Time, but it was a change I should not have made.

By the time in November 1996 Coventry decided to install Gordon as manager and make me director of football, I felt things were beginning to turn. Coventry were in the relegation zone and some of the football had been hopeless. But we had drawn our last five matches, there were an increasing number of players who could get you out of trouble and, finally, there was some solidity about the place.

As director of football, I scouted players, persuaded Roland Nilsson to come to Coventry from Helsingborg, where he'd gone after leaving Sheffield Wednesday, and watched some games. Gordon started slowly. He drew his first game, at Wimbledon, and lost the next three. A month into his reign, Coventry had ten points from sixteen matches. Then came a recovery with four straight wins, but by the time they were beaten by West Ham at home in March, Coventry were where they always seemed to be – in the relegation zone.

Gordon had appointed Alex Miller, who had played for Rangers and managed Hibernian, as his number two. Miller was, shall we say, not the kind of person to spread levity through a dressing room. Whenever I used to come into the canteen some of the players would come over to hear some gossip or a few jokes and one of them said, 'Have you noticed that Alex always walks out of the room when you come in?'

After the West Ham defeat, I took a call from John Motson, who had been commentating at Highfield Road. 'That club you are involved with are certainties to go down,' he said. 'You've got to get back in and do something.'

I went in to see Gordon. 'Look, Strach,' I said, 'I am told you're going to go down.'

'You might be right.'

'The next game is at Liverpool and you know what my record's like at Anfield. I can always get a result there. Why don't you take me with you?'

My record against Liverpool was good. When they were in their pomp when I was at Manchester United, we had only lost once to them in four years. Two seasons before, I'd taken Coventry to Anfield and we'd won 3–2 with Peter Ndlovu hitting a hat-trick. The previous season we'd fought out a goalless draw there. We would certainly take that now.

It was a Sunday game. Coventry were bottom, Liverpool were third, level on points with Arsenal and three behind Manchester United. They had games in hand on both. A win would take them top. We stayed at Haydock Park and on the Saturday evening I got the lads together for a sports quiz. We had a good laugh and travelled up the East Lancs Road to Anfield.

When we arrived, I ran into the Liverpool manager Roy Evans, who put his head in his hands and said, 'Oh, not the albatross.' Gordon said he would rather I didn't sit on the bench so I went to the Main Stand and watched McAllister give a masterclass, although we won courtesy of David James, who dropped two corners.

I was not asked again.

# SIXTEEN

I WAS IN THE CINEMA, WATCHING A FILM ABOUT THE PLACE
we used to call Rome. It was *The Full Monty*, the story of the Sheffield
steel workers who take to stripping as a way of making a living after
the blast furnaces closed. In one scene you could see the shop owned by
David Ford, who played for Sheffield Wednesday in the 1966 FA Cup
final. I'd always loved Sheffield, that other city built on seven hills, and
now it was to come into my life once more.

When we got back to our car, which had one of those phones that
looked like a house brick, I had a message to ring Dave Richards at
Sheffield Wednesday. David Pleat had been sacked as manager the day
before. I said to Maggie, 'Do you fancy going back to Rome?'

It was a continuation of my time at Coventry, only the location had
changed. Highfield Road had become Hillsborough. David Pleat had
been sacked after a 6–1 defeat at Manchester United that left Sheffield
Wednesday bottom of the Premier League in November 1997. It would
be another salvage job.

At the time I had arranged a meeting with Jim Boyce, the secretary
of the Northern Ireland FA, about managing the country's footballers
in the Euro 2000 qualifiers. I phoned Jim to tell him any deal was off,
but I did recommend Lawrie McMenemy, who took the job.

The job of an international coach is about selection, organisation and motivation. It is not about improving a player and it is probably best suited to an older manager. I had been sounded out about the England job after Graham Taylor's resignation in 1993 but I still hankered after the day-to-day involvement of club football. Later on the idea appealed more and I was asked about managing Turkey and South Africa.

The prospect of managing South Africa was particularly appealing and I flew out to Johannesburg to meet Danny Jordaan, the head of the South African FA. They were convinced they would be hosting the 2006 World Cup. Managing the World Cup hosts, who had players of the calibre of Benni McCarthy, Quinton Fortune, Mark Fish, Lucas Radebe and Aaron Mokoena, would have been quite a gig. In the end, they didn't get the World Cup and I didn't take the job.

International management suits some people but not others. When Glenn Hoddle was appointed by England, he was 38 and, although he very quickly proved himself an excellent and innovative coach, he simply had not developed the kind of man-management techniques you need to deal with as many egos as the average England dressing room possesses.

Franz Beckenbauer was a superb international manager, who took West Germany to two World Cup finals, but he never seemed to enjoy management at club level. He had a fractious time at Marseilles and then a couple of successful spells as caretaker at Bayern Munich, but at neither club was Beckenbauer able to stick it out for a season.

Enzo Bearzot, who took Italy to the 1982 World Cup, did very little at club level. His only management experience was in Serie C. You ask yourself if Bobby Moore would not have been better managing England rather than Southend, provided he had a decent backroom staff around him.

Had I taken the Northern Ireland job, my first game would have been against Turkey in the Ali Sami Yen. Instead, my first match as manager of Sheffield Wednesday was against Arsenal. They were a point off the summit of the Premier League, a competition they would win six months later. We beat them 2–0 at Hillsborough.

We lost only two of our first nine matches and, after a 2–1 win over Leeds, Sheffield Wednesday had climbed to eleventh by January 1998. Perhaps the highlight of the season followed a month later in the form of another epic encounter with Liverpool. It was played at Hillsborough on Valentine's Day, not long after Michael Owen had broken into the England side. He scored three and but for Kevin Pressman he might have had five. Benito Carbone scored with a beautiful lob, Paolo di Canio and Andy Hinchcliffe put Sheffield Wednesday 3–1 up and then Owen hit back. He was eighteen years old.

He had made his debut for England against Chile in midweek and as I prepared for the game I didn't think Liverpool would start with him. Owen would be tired, his head wouldn't be right. He did start and he was electricity itself. He was up against Des Walker, who was a very quick defender, and at times Owen was unplayable.

There was a lot made of England's Golden Generation but they only ever possessed two true international-class strikers in Michael Owen and Wayne Rooney, and I always argued they would win nothing if either of them got injured.

Because speed was such a part of his game, those injuries took more out of Owen than most players. I once talked to Tony Parkes, who was Blackburn's first-team coach for many years, and he told me that unless you really studied Alan Shearer you wouldn't know he was troubled by an injury.

Shearer's first significant injury at Blackburn, tearing his cruciate ligaments against Leeds in 1992, Tony said, took about 10 per cent off his top game. In each of his next three years at Ewood Park, he still managed thirty goals a season. In 1997, Shearer wrecked his ankle ligaments in a pre-season tournament at Goodison Park, which cost him that explosive pace in the box. He was never quite the same player again but he was still a formidable proposition.

Once Owen's pace began to falter after a series of injuries, his career fell away. He was not a good link-up player and neither was Robbie Fowler. He had not much else to offer. He scored two great goals in two

World Cups – 1998 and 2002 – that might have taken England to a final. The match against Argentina was lost on penalties and my memory of England chasing the game against Brazil was of Paul Scholes standing in the left-back position, hitting forty-yard balls to Rio Ferdinand, who had been pushed up front to try to disrupt the Brazilian defence. Frankly, I would have preferred it the other way around.

England should have built their team around Paul Scholes. He should have been our Cruyff and, if people had to be dropped to accommodate him, then so be it. Instead, Sven-Goran Eriksson was obsessed by David Beckham. Beckham, internationally, was a good player but Scholes was world class. Xavi Hernandez said he was the best central midfielder he had seen in the last twenty years. If my life depended on picking someone to score from ten yards out with the ball at his feet, I would choose Scholes.

He was part of the Manchester United team that came to Hillsborough in March 1998, seemingly certain to win the league. They were eleven points clear of Arsenal and, although they had lost Roy Keane to injury, the absence of their captain hadn't seemed to interrupt their rhythm.

One of my friends was a former waiter called Renato Pagliari, who was born in a village near Rome – the real Rome! – and had come to live in Sutton Coldfield. He was a wonderful tenor, had appeared on *New Faces* and had been paired up with a singer called Hilary Lester. Together they were known as Renee and Renato and their song 'Save Your Love' was the Christmas number one in 1982.

I'd got to know him because he was a big Aston Villa fan and I always maintained that only Luciano Pavarotti could sing 'Nessun Dorma' better than Renato. Because we had Benito Carbone and Paolo di Canio, I had the idea of bringing him into the dressing room before the United game. 'Come on, Lumpo,' which is what I used to call him, 'let's sing the Goalkeeper's Song.' We always called 'Nessun Dorma' the Goalkeeper's Song because the BBC footage that used the music for the 1990 World Cup climaxed with film of Dino Zoff making a full-length save.

And so he begins: '*Nessun dorma, nessun dorma. Tu pure o principessa, nella tua fredda stanza* . . .' I was standing by the door in the dressing room when Alex Ferguson walked past and I said to him, 'Come in and listen to this.' So he did and then Sheffield Wednesday's commercial manager followed him in and asked, 'If we gave him a microphone, would he do the song on the pitch?'

'You try to stop him,' I said.

Sheffield Wednesday won 2–0. Peter Atherton opened the scoring with a header and then Di Canio finished it all off with an overhead kick. Manchester United didn't seem too stung by the defeat. They were so far in front that Fergie was able to dismiss it as a blip.

But week by week, game by game, Arsenal kept eating into their lead. Later that month, Arsenal came to Old Trafford and won 1–0 and then they beat us by the same score at Highbury.

I'd used that match to give a debut to a kid from Macedonia called Goce Sedloski. He'd come to Wednesday from Dinamo Zagreb and I recommended that we kept him on. The board were against it, saying they were worried about his knees and that he was injury prone. Eight years later, he was man of the match when Macedonia came to Old Trafford and forced a goalless draw against England – one of the results that doomed their attempt to qualify for Euro 2008.

We were putting together a fairly decent team. Di Canio and Carbone were already there and, while Paolo required some careful handling, Benito was a great bloke, a proper professional and a marvellous talent.

When he came to Hillsborough, Di Canio was only ever going to be a short-term signing. If you look at his career, Di Canio never stayed anywhere for long. He was not particularly rated in Italy inasmuch as he did not win an international cap and he was at Sheffield Wednesday when I arrived there having fallen out with Celtic. You could never tell how Paolo would play, his demeanour before a match gave you no inkling whatsoever, but one thing you could always rely on was that there would be trouble whenever his agent was in town.

At times, he was electric – he scored fifteen goals in twenty-one games.

At times, he was anonymous. You would look out from the dug-out and think, 'Well, where is he?' For consistency Benito was vastly better but there were some games that Di Canio simply turned.

My last win as manager of Sheffield Wednesday was in late April at Everton. Di Canio scored twice and one was reminiscent of Ricky Villa's goal in the 1981 FA Cup final but on a far bigger scale. Di Canio took the ball on the halfway line, swept it past two defenders, and then dummied the keeper twice.

I called him the Volcano. I'd left Wednesday by the time he pushed over the referee, Paul Alcock, but the year before he had been a hair's breadth from doing the same.

We were playing Watford in an FA Cup replay at Hillsborough and Gary Willard was refereeing. There was a throw-in in the far corner; it may have been ours and it may have been theirs. It was a nothing decision but Di Canio starts arguing with the linesman and very soon he is in the referee's face. Willard books him for arguing with the linesman and he still carries on and you are thinking, 'This is a throw-in in their bottom third, what is there to argue about?' Willard sent him off and Carbone, to his credit, went over to Di Canio and said, 'You deserved that.'

That was on the Monday. We were playing at Elland Road on the Saturday. We trained at twelve on the Friday and finished at two so we could go straight to the hotel in Leeds.

I went to find Di Canio, who was sitting on a wall talking to one of our scouts, Lil Fuccillo, in Italian. Judging from the gestures the subject was the unfairness of it all. I went over to him and said, 'Shut up, Paolo, you should have been sent off.' And he simply walked away. The bus was supposed to have left for Leeds at four and nobody knew where he was. Eventually, we went without him.

I then got a call from a mutual Italian friend who said he knew where Paolo was and that he wanted a reconciliation. I said we had a pre-match meal at eleven and, if Paolo were there, he would be under consideration. If he wasn't, I would have no option but to leave him out.

He arrived during the meal and persuaded me to play him.

I'd love to tell you that he won the game single-handedly, driven on by all the points he had to prove. We did win the game as it happened but Paolo was so utterly hopeless we had to take him off.

I'd brought in Andy Hinchcliffe and Earl Barrett from Everton and Niclas Alexandersson from Gothenburg and then I got a call from an agent friend of mine in Manchester, Phil Black, asking if I would be interested in someone called Emerson Thome. I asked who he was.

'Well, Ron. He's a Brazilian centre-half, he's played in Portugal, he's been at Stoke with Chris Kamara and then he went to Huddersfield.'

'Why haven't any of these clubs signed him?'

'They haven't got the money and, anyway, when you see him, you'll love him.'

'I'll tell you what then, Blackie, you bring him to the training ground. We'll have a five-a-side and he's got five minutes. You stay in the car with the engine running and, if he's no good, you can put him straight back in the car. He's not even getting a shower.'

The car pulled up and out of it got this big, strapping lad with long hair. 'You're a handsome bastard,' I thought. Then he started playing and I shouted over to Phil Black, 'Switch the engine off.' We signed Emerson on a three-year contract and then sold him to Chelsea for £4m.

I had floated the idea of bringing Nigel Pearson back to Hillsborough. He was at Middlesbrough coming to the end of his playing career and was looking for a job in management. He could work under me, as Gordon Strachan had done at Coventry, and then take over.

Although Dave Richards has the reputation of being one of the least popular chairmen in Sheffield Wednesday's history, I'd always got on reasonably well with him and found him, to my face at least, reasonably supportive.

He had offered me a three-year contract when I'd arrived in November but I'd told him I would take a deal to the end of the season, in case we ended up being relegated. As it was, Sheffield Wednesday were out of trouble in a couple of months. After the Premier League season finished I was sent their offer of a new contract, which was for less money than I was already on. When I called him about it, he said, 'I told them you wouldn't accept it.'

That was on the Tuesday. I told him to come and see me on the Friday and we would sort out a new contract. The day before, his secretary rang to say Richards could not make the meeting. 'He does know I am going to Barbados on Sunday?' I asked.

The day before I was due to go on holiday, I was at Wembley commentating on the FA Cup final between Arsenal and Newcastle. As I was driving back from London, I had a phone call from Carlton Palmer. He was at Southampton but I'd agreed terms with him to come back to Sheffield, where he still lived, in the summer.

'Gaffer, is everything all right at your club?'

'I think so, why?'

'I've been with my solicitors about the move and they've been talking to Graham Mackrell (the Wednesday club secretary), who told them you aren't going to be here next season.'

I then rang Dave Richards, who loved the phrase: 'I'll tell it to you straight', which is a figure of speech I've always been suspicious of. At the other end of the phone, he wasn't telling it straight. He was evasive, incoherent and mumbling.

We flew off to the Caribbean and that was the last I heard from him. When I was out in Barbados I read reports that the club wanted Danny Wilson as their next manager. When I got home, I was phoned by Mackrell, who said he wanted me to return my company car.

I told him I would do it when Sheffield Wednesday paid me the bonus I had agreed for keeping them up, which was worth £100,000. Mackrell replied, 'I still want your car and could you bring the other one back as well.'

The club car was a Lexus but I'd been to the same dealer and bought myself a Toyota Land Cruiser. I asked Mackrell if I was supposed to give the club my own property as part of the severance package.

The next time I saw Dave Richards was two years later. We were in Malta where England were playing a friendly before Euro 2000. Sheffield

Wednesday had just been relegated from the Premier League, whose chairman was now Dave Richards.

'So, Dave, what happened at Sheffield Wednesday?'

'You turned down our offer of a new contract.'

'Did I hell.'

# SEVENTEEN

I WAS SITTING IN THE LONE STAR RESTAURANT IN BARBADOS, overlooking the sweep of sand and surf of the Atlantic, when the offer came in for my last big football job.

It was January 1999. I had just played golf and was sitting with, among others, Frankie Dettori when a fax arrived from Irving Scholar at Nottingham Forest asking me if I would like to manage the club. They were bottom of the Premier League. Their manager, Dave Bassett, had just been sacked and their leading asset, Pierre van Hooijdonk, had spent three months of the season on strike. Frankie and the rest of them kept saying, 'You can do it!' and I faxed back a heads of agreement from the restaurant.

The next fax I received detailed the remaining fixtures. The first three at home were: Arsenal, Manchester United and Chelsea. For the first one I sat in the wrong dugout. I went out waving to the crowd, posing for pictures, and then ducked my head and sat down next to Dennis Bergkamp, Nelson Vivas and Patrick Vieira.

I have been present when a manager has walked into the wrong dressing room. In May 1984, Manchester United were playing Ipswich at Old Trafford and were leading 1-0 at half time when Bobby Ferguson, who had been watching the game in the Main Stand, burst in and began shouting that the referee had been a disgrace and how they should 'start sorting out Bryan Robson'. After ten seconds he stopped, looked around and realised that 'his' players were wearing red shirts. Whatever Ferguson said when he got back to the away dressing room must have worked because Ipswich won 2-1. It was the last time Manchester United lost a league game at home after leading at the interval.

When I first started going to the City Ground as a manager, Brian Clough would always have his dugout on the halfway line. The visitors were right down the pitch towards the corner flag. In October 1980, they'd beaten us in a terrific match which finished 2-1. Afterwards, I was talking to Cloughie and Peter Taylor and I said, 'The visitors' dug-out is a joke.'

And Peter laughed knowingly: 'Yes, it is, isn't it?'

The following March, we played the return fixture. the Hawthorns was undergoing major renovation work. By the time Nottingham Forest arrived they had rebuilt half the main stand that included the dressing rooms and they had constructed the home team's under-cover dugout. The rest was mechanical diggers, JCBs and big, thick tyre tracks. They had also erected a temporary, away dug-out next to the home team one.

On the morning of the match, I said to some workmen, 'See that dug-out, take it up, move it to the far corner of the pitch and nail it down so it can't be moved. It pelted with rain, we won the game 2-1 and Clough and his staff had come squelching through the tyre tracks and the mud towards the dressing rooms. 'All right over there, was it?' I called out. The reply was unprintable.

Nottingham Forest in 1999 looked a bigger mess than a rainswept, half-built Hawthorns. Their last league win had been in August, five months before. A defeat in the FA Cup to Portsmouth in front of barely 10,000 at the City Ground had sealed Dave Bassett's fate as manager.

They had been promoted in May mainly because of Van Hooijdonk's 34 goals. He had then promptly gone on strike because he argued Forest had not strengthened the team and had sold his fellow centre-forward, Kevin Campbell, to Trabzonspor.

Van Hooijdonk had been persuaded back in November and when he scored against Derby with a flicked header, not one of his team-mates went over to celebrate with him. In terms of Dutch footballers, he was the polar opposite of Arnold Muhren. One was a model professional, Van Hooijdonk was a stroppy bastard.

When I first saw him I said, 'What you do will not affect my life one iota. If you are half as good as you think you are, you will be twice the player you actually are.'

He could either try to make a go of it at Nottingham Forest or not. I would not be lying awake at night thinking about it. When I brought Carlton Palmer to the club he said to Van Hooijdonk, 'We have all got to work and run and fight because, if we don't, there will be tears and the tears will be yours.'

He was brilliant at free-kicks and set plays. I once walked into the medical room at Forest where I overhead Larry Lloyd, who had been centre-half in the great European Cup winning sides, talking to our full-back, Alan Rogers. 'Can you tell me,' Larry was saying to Alan, 'why our six-foot-four centre-forward takes the free-kicks and corners?'

'Because he can't bloody head the ball,' said Alan.

'Spot on,' I said as I walked in.

When I introduced Marlon Harewood as his partner, he told Marlon that he didn't want him running the channels. 'That's exactly what I want him to do,' I said. 'He is young, he is quick, he is willing. Don't you dare tell him how to play.'

I'd been told there was a budget for players so, after selling Craig Armstrong to Huddersfield for £750,000, I bought Carlton from Southampton and then made an offer to Oxford for Dean Windass, because Nottingham Forest badly needed footballers who knew how to scrap for their lives. I was told the club would not sanction the transfer because, at thirty, Windass was 'too old'. Nine years later at Wembley he scored the goal that got Hull promotion to the Premier League.

Towards the end of April, when it was clear Forest were going to be relegated, I was preparing the team to play Aston Villa. A lot of my thoughts were centred on Steve Stone, who had come back from injury and started to play very well. I then picked up the phone to be told that Steve had been sold to Aston Villa for £6m.

It then dawned on me why I had been offered the job. I said to Peter Shreeves, who had come in as my assistant, 'We are here as damage limitation.' Had they delayed the appointment of a manager another week, the fans might have stormed the barricades. They had to have someone in and I was available.

I did make one signing. Richard Gough was 36 and had just returned from America, where he was playing for San Jose, and was looking for somewhere to train. I barely knew him but told him he could come down and train with us. He looked that good that I put him in the first team. His debut for us was marking Alan Shearer. Gough was nearly forty when he stopped playing at Everton.

After relegation, they sold Van Hooijdonk to Vitesse Arnhem for £3.5m, which together with the sale of Steve Stone should have given them a war chest to fund promotion under David Platt. Unfortunately, Platt, who was an aficionado of Italian football, blew the money on three Italians – Gianluca Petrachi, Salvatore Matrecano and Moreno Mannini. They managed 33 games between them and ripped a huge hole in the club's finances from which Nottingham Forest have never properly recovered.

Nottingham Forest was a lovely club. It just had nobody running it. The chairman was Nigel Wray, whose main sporting interest was Saracens rugby club and who, because of the abuse he was getting, did not come to the City Ground. In my months at Forest I never met him. The first time I ran into him was six years after I'd left on the night of the Champions League final in Istanbul.

I was in London hosting a tribute evening to three of the BBC's greatest commentators, Richie Benaud, Peter Alliss and Harry Carpenter. Somebody said, 'That's Nigel Wray over there.' So I went over and introduced myself to him. 'I used to manage your football club.'

'You were very complimentary about me,' he replied, because shortly after I'd left I'd written that 'although I've never met Nigel Wray, I understand he is a very nice man'.

I told him that a chairman who you never saw wasn't the worst relationship for a manager to have in football.

Wray employed Irving Scholar, a proper football man who had been chairman of Tottenham, to run the club. Unfortunately, Irving lived in Monaco. Brian Clough's secretary, Claire, was still at the club and I leaned on her as much as anyone.

The man himself was very supportive. Brian told me I should stay at Forest after they were relegated and bring them back up. He came to one or two games while I was there but he preferred to stay away on the grounds that his presence at the City Ground would be seen as a distraction. He didn't want to embarrass anyone.

Losing 8–1 at home to Manchester United was something of an embarrassment. Ole Gunnar Solskjaer scored four in a dozen minutes after coming on as a substitute. It was the heaviest home defeat ever suffered in the Premier League, beating Forest's 7–1 thrashing of Sheffield Wednesday at Hillsborough in 1995. You would have to go back to the day in 1908 Newcastle lost the Tyne–Wear derby 9–1 at St James' Park to find a worse home result in the English top flight.

Funnily enough, I may have been embarrassed but I wasn't furious. I told the press I was proud to have played my part in a nine-goal thriller. Manchester United were in their pomp. Three months later I would be at the Nou Camp to watch them secure the third leg of their astonishing Treble in the final of the Champions League. There was nothing much a club like Nottingham Forest could have done to stop them in that mood.

I was in charge for seventeen matches, from which we took a point a game, which wouldn't have been bad over the course of a season but was a fraction of what Nottingham Forest required. When I joined I joked that we needed to average around four points a game to survive.

When it was clear we were not going to survive, I wanted to put down some foundations for Forest's future. Marlon Harewood was nineteen, a product of the club's youth system, and I told him, 'You will play every game from now on, providing you don't freeze.' I'd done the same with Ugo Ehiogu at Aston Villa once we had won the League Cup. Villa in 1994 were not going to be relegated but they were not going to win anything either and this was a moment to give a young footballer an extended run.

There were only three young players I knew from the beginning would make the grade. One was Norman Whiteside and a second was Lee Hendrie.

When I was at Aston Villa, we would stay in a hotel before home games and then come into the training ground to work on a few set plays. Invariably, the youth team would be playing on a Saturday morning and people like Steve Staunton and Kevin Richardson would stop just to watch Hendrie play.

Hendrie graduated to the first team after I'd left the club and the mistake they made with him was to play him out of position. Lee's best position was on the left as the fourth midfielder, what I would call the 'John Robertson position' – not a quick winger but an extremely skilful left-sided player.

I watched him play in the FA Youth Cup against Tottenham. Lee was injured, he could barely run and he was being marked by Stephen Carr, who would go on to have a very good career at Spurs and Newcastle. Hendrie scored twice from out on the left.

Once he established himself in the first team, Villa began to play Hendrie as a central midfielder with Gareth Barry stationed outside him. The positioning had no logic to it. Neither was quick and Barry, relatively speaking, had no pace at all, but he was very good in the centre circle where he could go either way and where he could pass the ball intricately. Lee was far better on the flanks, where he could do a trick or isolate a defender, much like Marc Albrighton does for Leicester, although Lee had more craft and he could score a goal.

Lee also had something of a reputation as a playboy. I play golf with him now and again and I once told him, 'If I had still been your manager, I would have called you in and given you a smack around the head.' He once smashed his Porsche up trying to make it to Birmingham airport before one of Aston Villa's European games. I would have made him drive a Mini.

Lee was a smashing lad but he needed someone who could get a grip of him while at the same time not being too down on him. He needed to be encouraged.

What really disappointed me was when Martin O'Neill came to manage Villa in 2006. He had as his assistant John Robertson, who I thought should have opened up a school for wingers much as leading goalkeepers run goalkeeping schools. I thought Robertson would take Hendrie on and help him become the kind of player he himself had been at Nottingham Forest. But Lee ended up playing one league game for them before he was farmed out.

The third young player I knew instantly would make it was a young Manchester United midfielder called Aidan Murphy, who we were convinced would become the next Bryan Robson. He was a bursting, energised midfielder and at sixteen years of age he played for United's reserves against Nottingham Forest in the Central League.

Cloughie used to play quite a few first-teamers in those games. We put seven past them and Aidan scored four. Arnold Muhren was playing in that game for United and Aidan kept making the kind of runs that Arnold could just slot a pass to. He played against Manchester City in the 1986 FA Youth Cup final and he looked to be the jewel in that team.

The next season, Aidan went completely. I'd left Old Trafford in November and in the summer of 1987 he was sold to Crewe. He may have had problems mentally coming to terms with what was expected of him.

It is harder for young footballers now than it was then. The Under-2 1 league is not a patch on the old Central League. When Aidan scored his four goals against Nottingham Forest, he would have been playing alongside Arnold Muhren and Frank Stapleton, who would either be feeling their way back from injury or wanting to make a point as to why they should be in the first team.

In a Premier League dominated by foreign footballers that no longer happens as much and, if you are 21, you should in any case be pretty close to the first team. There is not a lot of value attached to winning the Under-21 league; to me the only youth trophy that carries real value is the FA Youth Cup.

Even then, reaching the final is not necessarily a sign that you are going be flooding the first team with young players. In 1991, when I was at Sheffield Wednesday, we lost the FA Youth Cup final to Millwall after beating Manchester United in the semis. Although it was an achievement, I didn't see too many Wednesday players I thought were going to make it for us. There were one or two who I thought would make a living in the game but not in the top flight.

We reached two Youth Cup finals in my time at Manchester United. The one in 1982 had five who we thought were going to make it: Mark Hughes, Norman Whiteside, Graeme Hogg, Clayton Blackmore and Nicky Wood, who could have had a glittering career at Old Trafford but for a serious back injury. Four years later, aside from Aidan, there were only two we would bet on and, although Lee Martin scored the goal that won the 1990 FA Cup, neither he nor Gary Walsh really established themselves at Old Trafford.

Chelsea have won the Youth Cup five times in seven years but, although they have very high hopes for Kasey Palmer, those players have not formed the bedrock of the first team in the way the Class of '92 did for Manchester United.

Nottingham Forest was my last club. From now on I would be part of the media, looking in from the outside. I was sixty; I had signed a contract with ITV. It was a new chapter, a new adventure.

# EIGHTEEN

THE BEGINNING OF MY ASSOCIATION WITH ITV WAS MUCH happier than its end. It was December 1978 and I was standing in the snow at Old Trafford being interviewed by Gerald Sinstadt, who was Granada's lead commentator. I was standing next to the Manchester United manager, Dave Sexton. We had won 5–3 in one of the finest and best-remembered performances in West Brom's history. Perhaps because of that, I may have been a bit brash.

What I said caught the ear of Paul Doherty, who was one of the most innovative sports producers in television. He became head of sport at Granada and pioneered a version of Sky's *Soccer Saturday* long before Jeff Stelling appeared on our screens. Had he not fallen out with so many people, he could and should have run ITV Sport.

He phoned me and said he had seen the interview and would I fancy doing some commentary? Bobby Charlton had been doing commentary for the BBC and he, like many summarisers of that generation, simply told you what you had just seen.

'I want it different,' said Paul. 'I want somebody who will come in and tell us why something has happened and what might happen. I want you to talk: "bang, bang, bang," and, if there's any action in the penalty area, stop talking. I want you to be quick and I want you to be concise.'

His father, Peter, was one of the finest footballers ever produced by Northern Ireland. He had won the championship with Manchester City in 1937 and, nine years later, the FA Cup with Derby. He had managed Northern Ireland to the quarter-finals of the 1958 World Cup.

His son was a passionate and uncompromising character. I once said to Paul, 'You need us, you need football.'

He replied, 'Ron, we could put an old movie on, a cowboy movie, and it would draw the same audience as a league match. We don't need you. We cover football for the prestige of it.'

My first prestige event was the 1980 European Championships in Italy. The Euros were not then the big tournament they have become. There were two groups of four teams and whichever country topped their group would proceed to the final.

The final match of Group A saw West Germany face Greece in Turin. However, just before kick-off, news came through that Holland and Czechoslovakia had drawn at the San Siro, which meant the Germans would qualify for the final without kicking a ball.

Suddenly, there were wholesale changes in the West German team as they looked to rest players for the final in Rome. They were even replacing players during the warm-up. Those who would be going to the final were not going to do anything that might result in their getting injured or suspended. Greece, who had barely won a corner in the whole tournament, were delighted with the prospect of a draw and a very tedious, goalless version began to play itself out at the Stadio Communale.

After five minutes I had said everything I could think of about the game. Paul Doherty, who was sitting beside me, began mouthing, 'Say something!' and then dug me in the ribs. I still couldn't think of anything worthwhile, although I was by now feeling the pain of the audience back home.

The England manager, Ron Greenwood, was supposed to have been doing the commentary for the final but he had fallen out with the media so badly during the tournament that he refused to do it, which meant I was kept on.

Even when I had done six or seven tournaments I would ring Paul to ask him how he thought I'd done. 'I quite liked that,' he'd say, picking out a phrase that he'd remembered. Then, of course, he would add, 'But why did you go on about that? What were you thinking of?'

My first game of that tournament also featured Greece, who were playing Czechoslovakia in the Olympic Stadium in Rome in front of 4,000. Martin Tyler was the lead commentator for the game and I remember sitting with him in the Cavalieri Hilton, which has wonderful views over the old city.

We were phonetically spelling out the names of the players and two I remember from the Greek team were Nikos Anastopoulos and Christos Ardizoglou. We kept writing them down and repeating them: 'ANNA-STOPOO-LOSS', 'HARDY-ZOG-LOO'. It was just as well because Anastopoulos scored with a header and just before I'd said, 'If the Czechs aren't careful, he's going to nick one.'

My regular commentator was Brian Moore, the epitome of an English gentleman, who adored cricket as much as he did football. Just before the final we watched the two teams, Belgium and West Germany, training.

One of the stars of the Belgian side was Wilfried van Moer, who had broken his leg against Italy in the 1972 tournament. That was it for his international career until he was called up for two must-win games against Portugal and Scotland that qualified Belgium for the European Championships. He was 35.

As we were chatting to him, Van Moer said, 'I love English football. I even run a bar called Wembley in my home town.' As he said it, Mooro dug me in the ribs and said, 'Keep that to yourself.' However well-mannered and polite he may have been on the screen, Brian was first and foremost a journalist and he wanted stories. The bar is still there in Hasselt, northeast of Brussels.

For me the player of the tournament was Bernd Schuster, the blond 21-year-old midfielder whose performances for Cologne and West Germany would earn him a transfer to Barcelona once the championships were done.

During half-time, when the studio panel were live, we were discussing the game among ourselves, although the relay meant the studio could hear what we were saying. Mooro said, 'Schuster reminds me forcibly of Alan Hudson when he first started playing for Chelsea. I can't believe I haven't mentioned it in commentary.'

'Are you having a laugh,' I said. 'You've only got to look at him; blond, German, central midfield, European Championship. He is a ringer for Gunter Netzer in the 1972 tournament.'

During the second half when we were back live, Schuster played a lovely ball to Horst Hrubesch and Brian said to the audience, 'I can't believe how much Bernd Schuster reminds me of the great Gunter Netzer, don't you agree, Ron?'

'No, Brian, to me he seems more like Alan Hudson when he started playing for Chelsea.'

Mooro was a wonderful commentator who let the game breathe. He did not let his commentary become over-technical, he knew the value of silence and he did not become hysterical in high-pressure moments.

I also commentated with Peter Brackley and we did the opening game of the 1986 World Cup, but the feeds had been put in the wrong socket so our commentary was delivered to the good people of Burma.

Brian retired after the 1998 World Cup final and died three years later on the night Michael Owen scored his hat-trick against Germany in Munich. I was just watching Owen coming off the pitch when I took a call from a newspaper asking for my reaction to Brian's death.

His successor, Clive Tyldesley, is a wonderful observer of the game, not tactically but of things that are happening around you. His finest hour was the 1999 Champions League final. 'Can United score, they always score,' just as Teddy Sheringham was about to hit Manchester United's injury-time equaliser and then: 'Name on the trophy,' when the ball hit the net.

Bayern Munich had so dominated that game the only surprise was that Manchester United were only trailing by a single goal. In the 86th minute Carsten Jancker hit the crossbar with an overhead kick and I said,

'That could be the moment Manchester United win the European Cup.'

It was a strange, surreal occasion. I don't think Bobby Charlton saw the United goals because he had gone down in the lift with the UEFA presentation party with the trophy, which had Bayern Munich's colours tied to it. George Best had disappeared into the night.

I had to pick the man of the match just before the final went into stoppage time and the shortlist was all from Munich – Lothar Matthaus, Jens Jeremies and Mario Basler. Curiously, Ottmar Hitzfeld had substituted Matthaus and Basler when Sheringham equalised. We didn't actually award a man of the match because everything changed so completely. It was that kind of night.

Sometimes, when mixing with the players you were commentating on, there would be embarrassing moments. I found myself in the England team hotel in Mexico City immediately after they had been knocked out by Maradona's Hand of God. I was Manchester United manager then and was talking to Bryan Robson and Gary Bailey when Peter Shilton came over to me.

'Why didn't you sign me for United?' he said, completely oblivious to the fact that Gary was standing directly behind me.

'Well, I've got to tell you that we have had the best defensive record in the league for the last three seasons, Peter.'

'If you'd have signed me, you would have won everything in sight.'

'Oh, come on, you nugget, you know that's nonsense. Anyway, are you telling me you're the best goalkeeper in the world?'

'I am the best in the world.'

'The best keeper in the world would have stopped that first goal of Maradona's. The best goalkeeper in the world would have made sure he got to the ball before Maradona.'

During that time, I didn't just use the microphone for commentating. In 2002, I appeared at Ronnie Scott's singing a selection of Sinatra standards.

They had opened a sister club to the one in London on Broad Street in Birmingham. It closed a few years ago to become a lap-dancing venue, but then there was a real buzz about the place and Gary Newbon wanted to use the premises to stage a charity event run by Princess Diana's brother, Charles Spencer.

Gary had called me and said, 'You like a song, will you do a few numbers? Terry Venables will do something and so will Dion Dublin.' Jasper Carrott would do the compering.

I said I couldn't see any problem with that and promptly forgot about it. Some time later, I was driving along Broad Street, past Ronnie Scott's, when I saw a billboard that said, 'Big Ron Pays Tribute to Sinatra'. I would be paying my tribute in around three weeks' time.

I phoned Newbon: 'You are having a laugh with this.'

'You'll do it, though, won't you?'

'I don't see that I've got much option.'

One of my neighbours was Cedric Whitehouse, who had worked with Chaka Khan, Roy Orbison and Kenny Rogers, and he put together an eight-piece band which featured Steve Gibbons, a great old rocker from Birmingham, and Ruby Turner, a fabulous soul singer who grew up in Handsworth and has sung with Mick Jagger, Bryan Ferry and Jools Holland.

Andy Townsend booked the entire front row and took up all the boys with him. 'If you are crap, we are going to slaughter you,' were his parting words.

I went to Ronnie Scott's in the afternoon for a sound check and listened in the empty theatre transfixed to Ruby singing 'I'd Rather Go Blind'. I thought to myself, 'I have got to follow this. What will they think?'

It worked out. I did five or six Sinatra numbers: 'Come Fly with Me', 'Lady Is a Tramp', 'That's Life' and 'New York, New York' with Ruby for an encore.

Charles Spencer liked it so much that he invited us to a private dinner party at Althorp, where he was entertaining fifty guests, and Ruby and I did a cabaret spot from the sweeping staircase.

# NINETEEN

IT IS JUST AFTER HALF PAST TEN IN MONACO ON AN APRIL night in 2004. Chelsea have blown their chance of a first Champions League final and I am about to blow my commentary career with a phrase I shall always regret.

The broadcast finished a few minutes ago. Chelsea, facing a Monaco side down to ten men, have lost the first leg of their semi-final 3–1. Realistically, there is no way back for them. My microphone has been slung away. It is a couple of yards from where I am sitting, mulling over the game. Out of the corner of my eye I see the highlights tapes going round, preparing them to be relayed to the studio. In the studio, they are on an ad break.

Normally, one of the production team will go over and switch off the microphones and disconnect the feeds. But tonight she doesn't. She heads straight to the tunnel, a place where she has no real business to be. I don't know why she went there. Perhaps she wants to take in the atmosphere around the dressing rooms. But the microphones are on and some of the feeds are still live. One is going to Dubai and, from there, across the Middle East.

Then, when Marcel Desailly appeared on the tape, I make my comment: 'He is what is known in some schools as a thick, lazy nigger.'

That is the only time I am going to say that word. It was a word I had never used before and have never used since. It was idiotic, stupid and offensive and I should never have said it. To this day, I cannot believe I did.

The one thing I can say in my defence was that I was quoting a phrase that at least two managers I knew had used. I didn't shout it; I almost mumbled it, with my head resting on my hand. I don't even think Clive Tyldesley, who was commentating with me, heard it. But in Dubai, via the open mike, they did.

I was furious with the way Chelsea had played. They should have romped the game. Every big team had gone out of the Champions League. There was just Monaco, Porto, Deportivo La Coruna and Chelsea left.

Monaco's main striker was Fernando Morientes, who was on loan from Real Madrid and who had scored the goal that had knocked out Madrid earlier in the competition. I said live on air that this was a big game for Marcel Desailly. He was a World Cup winner playing alongside John Terry, who was then 23. 'Desailly has got to help John Terry out,' I said.

Instead, Desailly kept trying to play offside with no account of where Terry was. Desailly was finishing at the end of the season, he would be going to Qatar and he had played like it.

When we left the Stade Louis II, I got a car back to the hotel with Frank Lampard's father. As we were being driven to the hotel, Frank Senior got a call from his son, who was raging about Chelsea's performance. Frank, like me, could not understand why his manager, Claudio Ranieri, had brought on Juan Sebastian Veron, who had barely played for the club that season, and left Joe Cole, who was a regular, on the bench. He was also scathing about Desailly's performance.

When we got to the hotel, I had a drink with Alec Stewart, who is a big Chelsea fan, and Robbie Williams, who I knew from when I'd appeared on *TFI Friday* with Chris Evans.

The storm broke the next morning. Normally, I would have flown back straight after the game but because it was Monaco I'd taken Maggie with me and we were sitting in the main square outside the hotel when Andy Townsend came over to me and said, 'We've got a bit of a problem, gaffer. Something's happened last night and they've got it on tape.'

I could not for the life of me imagine what he was talking about. 'What do you mean, got it on tape?'

Maggie was sitting with me and I was so confused that moments afterwards she said, 'You do realise you have just blanked Roman Abramovich?'

The man who owned Chelsea and whose yacht was moored in Monaco's harbour had come over to our table but we'd all got up to discuss this tape recording and he had moved away.

I was told that Brian Barwick, the head of ITV Sport, wanted a conference call with me and Clive Tyldesley immediately. Barwick had taken the job just before the 1998 World Cup and I first met him when he sat next to me when France played South Africa in Marseilles. Without question, Barwick had a huge leaning towards Liverpool and if I had been the former manager of Liverpool rather than Manchester United, I suspect he would not have finished me over the Desailly Affair.

Not long into the call I said, 'Right, I will resign.'

'Well,' Barwick said, 'if you are going to do that, then we had better have a chat in about three or four weeks' time.' The inference I drew from that was that ITV would have me back. But that was never on his agenda.

At the time my mind was racing back to all the players I'd worked with: Cyrille, Brendon and Laurie at West Brom when racism was at its height in the English game; Paul McGrath, Paul Williams, Carlton Palmer – people I am still friendly with now.

I was ashamed of what I'd said but the attitude of the black footballers I had worked with was the same. When contacted by the media, they insisted that what I had said was wrong but I was not a racist. In one game as manager of Aston Villa, I had played an entire team of black players with the exception of Mark Bosnich and Shaun Teale.

Neither Barwick nor ITV pointed any of that out to the media. They did not say I had been quoting a phrase. Before he joined ITV, I was never particularly close to Des Lynam because when he was with the BBC he was so convinced of how superior the corporation was to ITV. But he was very supportive now and he said I should have sued ITV because I was not working when I used the phrase and it was their error that it had been broadcast.

By the time we got back, the press was camped outside the front door and through them all came one of the area's most prominent businessmen, who was Indian. He had never been to our house in his life but he brought a bunch of flowers. He said, 'Ron, I am so sorry about what's happened. We all remember when you put the black boys in at West Brom.'

I am more aware of racism now than I was then. There are a lot of black players in the game but when I go to football functions I don't see too many black faces. Equally, when Diane Abbott made her comment about how 'white people love to divide and rule', I think that is equally racist.

The fall-out was long. One of the things it cost me was the chance to manage in the World Cup. I'd been approached by Jack Warner to take Trinidad and Tobago to the 2006 tournament in Germany. They had two qualifying games left, both very winnable. As it turned out I would have been managing Trinidad against England in Nuremberg.

But as soon as the appointment was announced, there were objections, some from a few players, including Dwight Yorke, and from the media. Warner said he wanted to let bygones be bygones and I had a contract, but eventually we agreed to let it go and Leo Beenhakker took the team to Germany. I could have sued the Trinidad FA but what was the point? I would probably still be in court now.

As the affair lingered, I was approached by Adrian Chiles, who had his own production company and was presenting *Match of the Day 2*. He wanted to do a film about the Desailly Affair called *What Ron Said*. He had approached Jeff Farmer, who Barwick had replaced as head of ITV Sport. Jeff thought it might help and there was a connection in that Chiles was a big West Brom fan.

Terry Venables had called me and suggested I stop apologising, and perhaps I should have listened to him. But I wanted to go in front of a television camera and tell people that, whatever they thought of me, I was not and never had been a racist.

The film that emerged from it was vacuous nonsense. I was taken back to the stadium in Monaco. I went to a radio station in America's Deep South where I was 'put on trial' and listened to some rednecks calling in, telling me in a southern drawl, 'There's nothing wrong with what you did.' Then I was taken to a museum of racist memorabilia in Birmingham, Alabama. There were golliwogs and a machine where you put a penny in and a black boy would play the drums.

Halfway through, I asked myself what on earth I was doing here. If it hadn't have been so serious, I would have been in stitches. The producer of the film was black and I think the expectation among the crew was that we would fall out big time. In actual fact, we got on very well, but I don't think the end results justified her efforts.

A few years later I did *Wife Swap*, which Maggie was dead against. I knew that I would be asked to pair up with a black woman because, after the Desailly Affair, they would think it would make good television. I was convinced I would be introduced to Diane Abbott.

Instead, I spent four days with Tessa Sanderson, who I had known when she was making her breakthrough in Wolverhampton. Afterwards, she invited us to her wedding. They were expecting a confrontation but my first words were: 'Hello, Tess, how's it going?'

When I became involved with Peterborough in 2006, things were not going well at all and they didn't become much better.

I'd been asked to do a series for Sky called Big Ron Manager in which I would use my expertise to troubleshoot at clubs who were in difficulties. Sky would pay the club £100,000 although the value to the clubs themselves in terms of exposure was worth far, far more.

The first club we approached was Swindon Town but, although the commercial staff were very keen, the manager, Iffy Onuora, was far less enthusiastic about the idea. We were given more and more restrictions as to where and when we could film and eventually Sky pulled the plug.

I suggested that they approach Peterborough, where Barry Fry was the owner. Barry had remortgaged his house to keep the club going and he said afterwards that the series saved Peterborough.

It was not just the £100,000. I helped them raise another £50,000 from a golf day and, much more importantly, the series was seen by the father of Darragh McAnthony, who called his son and told him to watch it. McAnthony, an Irish entrepreneur who was living in Spain, bought the club and took them into the Championship.

When I came to Peterborough, their attempt to get into League One via the play-offs was faltering. Their manager, Mark Wright, had been sacked and his assistant, Steve Bleasdale, had been pushed up to take his place. Initially, he had done quite well but now the wheels were coming off big time.

The biggest problem was the one swirling around their most talented young player, Sean St Ledger. They would be playing Macclesfield on Saturday and Celtic and Blackburn were interested in the centre half. Steve Bruce was looking to take him to Birmingham and scouts from all three clubs would be coming to London Road to watch him.

On the training session on the Friday morning, Bleasdale told St Ledger he would be playing at right back which left him totally unimpressed. St Ledger walked off the pitch. Barry got to hear of it, thought Bleasdale was undermining his chances of selling St Ledger, and went absolutely barmy.

When he phoned me, every second word began with 'f'. I told him to calm down and that we would meet with the television cameras at twelve o'clock at the ground. I was there with Jim Walker, my old physio from Aston Villa. Steve Bleasdale was lying on the sofa and his assistant, Andy Legg, was in the room.

Barry was standing up saying, 'I am picking the fucking team but I want input from all of you.'

'This is wrong,' I said. 'If you want to pick the team, then fine, but you can't have six people putting their two-penn'orth in. You have to have two people maximum.'

Bleasdale was rolling his eyes at this so I turned to him and said, 'Are you all right with that, Steve? Because, if you are not you cannot go into the dressing room with body language like that. The players will sniff it out immediately.'

I went out of the room and sat in the dug-out with Andy Legg. It was one o'clock, there was nobody in the ground and Andy turned to me and said, 'Something's up. If the captain and centre-half go out on the pitch, there will be something up because they know Steve well. They used to travel down with him from Liverpool.' Sure enough, the two men did appear.

I went back into the dressing room with the cameras. My rule was that I never said anything unless I was asked. Barry was giving his team talk and then Steve Bleasdale interrupted him.

I thought he was going to discuss a throw-in or something else they had been working on which would have surprised me because in all my time there I never saw Peterborough work on anything.

'Can I say something,' said Bleasdale. 'I resign fellas. Good luck everyone. See you later.' He then walked out.

As the door closed, Barry said, 'Life is full of pleasant surprises. Half of you didn't like him anyway.'

He left me to finish the team talk. I told them that from what I had seen they liked playing football and that they should go out and have some fun. Meanwhile, Steve Bleasdale was driving out of the ground, past the fans, stopping to text Barry Fry his resignation. When he got back to Liverpool, his wife slaughtered him for resigning without arranging any kind of pay-off.

Peterborough won 3-2. Danny Crow, who was a good little striker who might have achieved more in the game, scored in the 94th minute. In terms of points per game, I left London Road as Peterborough's most successful manager.

The only thing worth going on *Celebrity Big Brother* in 2013 for was the money. It was boring to film, let alone watch – I have never seen it – but it was extremely lucrative. I'd phoned up Razor Ruddock, who'd been on it, and he said, 'Ron, this is the easiest money you will ever earn. It's a walk in the park; it's like pre-season.'

I didn't know many of the other celebrities apart from Carol McGiffin from *Loose Women*. I was always aware that I was wearing a mike – after what happened in Monaco how could I not be? As a result I became the most boring bastard anyone channel-hopping could have stumbled across.

You are not supposed to have your phone on 24 hours before the show and we were all put up in a hotel five minutes away from the Big Brother House. I was the last one to be called but I wanted to phone Maggie and I told the girl who had come to collect me that I had to watch a football match because I would be reporting on it.

There was no football match but I watched the first few minutes of *Celebrity Big Brother*, which featured three of the contestants who had been 'hidden away'. They were the dancer Louie Spence, Sophie Anderton, a lingerie model who was once Mark Bosnich's girlfriend, and Lauren Harries, who as a curly-haired ten-year-old boy went on the *Wogan* show in a bow-tie discussing antiques. He had since become a woman.

They were together in a room discussing who they would be joining and when my name came up, Louie Spence said, 'Ron Atkinson? I don't think I'd have three words to say to him.'

When he came on, I went straight over to him and said, 'Louie, how wonderful to see you. I love your work.' Every time we were remotely in the same room I would go over and try to engage him in conversation. He simply did not want to know.

The three I got on best with were Charlotte Crosby, who won the whole thing, a lad called Abz Love, who was in a Simon Cowell boy band, and Bruce Jones, who had played Les Battersby in *Coronation Street*. As friendships, they weren't particularly long or particularly deep. I only lasted eight days.

# TWENTY

I WAS SITTING IN LIVERPOOL'S ANGLICAN CATHEDRAL LIS-
tening to Bill Kenwright deliver the address at Howard Kendall's
funeral and I began to wonder what had happened to men like the
Everton chairman, who represented the English businessman or
entrepreneur who owned the football club they grew up supporting.

People like Kenwright would back their manager with time and,
if they had it, money. They would know the realistic expectations of
what their club could achieve and they would expect them to develop
their own players.

I can understand someone like Manuel Pellegrini coming to Manchester City and having little real interest in the youth team or the
academy because they know they have a three-year contract they will
probably be lucky to see out and that the youth team or the academy
is someone else's province. They will still be there when the manager
has signed his name to a document that contains the phrase 'by mutual
agreement'.

When Arsene Wenger finally walks away from the Emirates Stadium,
will the Arsenal board look around for the best young British manager
in the country and appoint, for argument's sake, Eddie Howe from
Bournemouth? Or will they go to the circle of *galactico* coaches, who

always seem to be on hand when a big club needs a manager? I think you know the answer.

In the 1980s, there was a real desire in La Liga to bring in English mangers. Terry Venables went to Barcelona, I went to Madrid, Howard Kendall to Bilbao. Before he was appointed England manager, the best Sam Allardyce could have hoped for in the Premier League would be to dig a Sunderland or a Blackburn out of trouble, something he did more successfully than Remi Garde at Aston Villa or Pepe Mel at West Bromwich Albion.

Imagine for a moment that Steve Bruce were Spanish and had played centre-half for Real Madrid rather than Manchester United. Instead of managing Birmingham, Sunderland, Wigan and Hull, say he coached Espanyol, Athletic Bilbao, Getafe and Real Betis with some success. It seems inconceivable that Bruce would not at some stage be offered the chance to take charge at the Bernabeu.

There seems very little prospect of Bruce becoming Manchester United manager, even if Jose Mourinho's time at Old Trafford is brief, and you ask yourself why. Steve Bruce knows intimately how Manchester United operate, he would have an immediate rapport with the supporters.

People might say United tried that with David Moyes, but I don't think David ever really came to terms with the size of Manchester United or with the fact that they thought he should be transforming the club in one season.

Moyes had signed a six-year contract and he put far too much faith in that bit of paper. There was a clause in that document that he had to qualify Manchester United for the Champions League. The club could have let that go but, ultimately, they did not want him enough.

Moyes had done a brilliant job at Everton, in particular when it came to scouting and identifying players. My biggest regret about David was that he seemed far too apologetic about the fact he was not Alex Ferguson. He should have stood up and said, 'I am the manager of Manchester United. I am here because I am good enough and in six years I will transform this club.' He should have imposed himself on Old Trafford from the beginning, but he kept arguing that Manchester United were in transition. Manchester United could not be in transition, they were champions of England.

Shortly after I became Manchester United manager, I was having lunch in an Italian restaurant with a journalist called Bob Driscoll. He said, 'I can't believe you're so relaxed, sitting here in a restaurant chatting away when you're manager of Manchester United.'

I said, 'Of course I am relaxed. I am manager of Manchester United and I am good enough. I am quite looking forward to it.' It is a much bigger job than it was in 1981 but you still have to savour it and I don't think David did.

Manchester United always patted themselves on the back about how they had backed Alex Ferguson during three-and-a-half very thin years. They gave his successor eight months and you wonder how much time Fergie would have been given now.

Bluntly, Fergie would have failed to have qualified Manchester United for the Champions League in three of his first four full seasons. He was saved by the FA Cup. By the time Louis van Gaal won it in his final match for Manchester United, the FA Cup was no longer enough.

Jose Mourinho is the third full-time successor to Alex Ferguson and, if he can make two good signings, Manchester United might not be very far off the pace. The club needs, craves, a Ruud van Nistelrooy or even a Robin van Persie as he was in his first season at Old Trafford. Someone who will guarantee you twenty goals a season. Yes, Mourinho will inherit Anthony Martial and Marcus Rashford, two tremendous talents, but young footballers are prone to blips, especially in their second season.

The first time I met Mourinho was at Old Trafford in March 2004. It was the night he would knock Manchester United out of the European Cup and slide down the pitch in his suit. Normally, when I was commentating with ITV I would look at the opposition when they were warming up and see if I could talk to someone when they came off the pitch.

The trouble with Porto was that I wasn't sure who many of their players were. But Mourinho, who was standing by the tunnel, came over, introduced himself and said if I were ever in Portugal to look him up.

However, I have never been a fan of the siege mentality he looks to introduce to his clubs; trying to instil the belief that it is them against the world. Yes, you have to protect your players, but that does not mean you have to antagonise everybody else while doing it. I don't think that would work at Manchester United because it can lead to the club becoming unhealthily claustrophobic.

Something like that seems to have happened in his final season at Chelsea. Manchester United are a much bigger club than Chelsea. When tourists come to Manchester, Old Trafford is usually the first of their sights to visit in a way that Stamford Bridge isn't for tourists coming to London. It is a global brand and you cannot run it as your personal fiefdom. Manchester has another football focus five miles away in the shape of Pep Guardiola and Manchester City.

I don't think his treatment of the club doctor, Eva Carneiro, helped him but I don't think it was the root cause of Chelsea's collapse as some people have suggested. When they won the title, Chelsea limped rather than stormed over the line, and while Mourinho spent money in the summer of 2015, it was on footballers who disappeared without trace.

Radamel Falcao and Pedro made no real impact while Michael Hector was bought from Reading and promptly loaned back. So you ended up with the same players who had finished the previous season with momentum draining out of them, who were in a claustrophobic dressing room and who were probably annoyed about the treatment handed out to the club doctor on the opening day of the season. That is a recipe for a collapse.

Fergie at his peak was very good at getting one big-name signing per summer to Old Trafford. One year it would be Van Nistelrooy, another it would be Juan Sebastian Veron, the year after it would be Rio Ferdinand. One big player a year would not unbalance the squad but it would refresh it. It was a simple formula and it worked.

Football has changed over time but not as much as you might think. I sometimes tell young people, 'George Best was as good as Lionel Messi,' and they look at you as if you're deranged. You point out that Messi does not have to play against footballers who are out to maim him. Week in and week out Best would be up against one or two footballers who had been told to physically impose themselves on him, and some took the definition of 'physically impose yourself' to its very outer limits. You tell them that Best scored six goals at Northampton on a pitch that was fit only for a hippopotamus and they will roll their eyes.

I could once have brought George Best back to Manchester United. It was September 1981 and I had just taken over at Old Trafford. Best was in California, playing for San Jose Earthquakes. He would have been about 35 and was driven by the thought he might play for Northern Ireland in the World Cup in Spain. The highlight was a fabulous goal against Fort Lauderdale in which he beat half a dozen players.

George had been promoting a book in Manchester and in an interview with Radio Piccadilly he was asked whether he would be interested in ever coming back to United now they had a new manager. 'I would jump at the chance,' came the reply.

Radio Piccadilly then rang me at my office at the Cliff. 'George Best has just been on saying he would love to play for you.'

'Well, I know George and I've always been a fan and, if George can do it, I'd be more than interested and I'd certainly like to see him in training,' I said. 'The offer to come and train with us is there.'

I was sceptical but I rang George. We were playing Arsenal at Highbury and I told him that, if he were interested, I'd meet him at the Royal Garden Hotel on Kensington High Street at eight o'clock on Saturday evening.

George went to the game and saw us play out a terrible goalless draw and I went over to Kensington with a mate. 'What time are we seeing Bestie?' he said.

'My guess would be that we're not, but I will give him until one minute past eight,' I said. Needless to say, he didn't turn up.

What constitutes good football changes not just with time but with where you are. When I was working in Madrid, I was sent a tape of what I was assured was a classic match that Arsenal and Tottenham had just played.

Atletico had an away game and I put it on in the coach for the team to watch. As we were going along I thought, 'This isn't very good.' So I called over one of our defenders, Tomas Renones, to ask what he thought of the game. After a while Tomas shrugged his shoulders and said with a sigh, '*Mister, muchas disputas.*' He thought it was far too aggressive.

A lot of that has been lost from the English game and to me that's a matter for regret. I would rather see full-blooded challenges than shirt-pulling. When you saw Pepe rolling around on the ground pretending he had been punched in the face by Yannick Carrasco in the Champions League final between Real and Atletico, you hear people yearn for the old values. One friend of mine, who is a football fanatic, told me, 'This is the sort of thing that is turning me off the game.'

That kind of thing isn't new. Rodney Marsh was a past master at tripping himself up in the penalty area. He was great at manoeuvring the ball in the box but he was also great at putting one of his legs behind the other at speed and going over in the area. Whenever we came across him I would have a word with the referee. 'Remember what he's good at,' I'd say.

Most of my football life has been spent in the Midlands and in the spring of 2016 Midlands football had one of its greatest stories. Leicester City won the Premier League from starting odds of 5,000−1.

It was, however, one of the poorest Premier Leagues I can remember. I went to far too many matches where I was simply bored, and I don't get bored easily watching football.

Because of what Pep Guardiola achieved with Barcelona, possession football became the great mantra of the game. It is easy to see why − if you have the ball, the opposition can't score.

But because not every team plays like Barcelona, the principles became distorted, so you ended up with centre-halves passing the ball repeatedly to each other. One of the most damning criticisms of Manchester United under Louis van Gaal was how long they took to move the ball forward.

When people talk of the 'Manchester United way', they imagine the club has always been about flying wingers crossing the ball to fabulous centre-forwards. There were times when Manchester United were a long way from the peaks they climbed under Matt Busby and Alex Ferguson, but they have always been about high-tempo football. Old Trafford demanded it.

When you managed a team at Manchester United you would always tell your players just before they went out that the first twenty minutes would be crucial because you would have to contain a side that would be going for your throat from the off. When I was in the home dugout at Old Trafford I would often say, 'The crowd's expecting this, don't disappoint them.'

Right from the moment of Louis van Gaal's first game as Manchester United manager, a 2–1 home defeat by Swansea, the tempo was hardly ever there. The two players who spent more time on the ball under Van Gaal than any other were Chris Smalling and Daley Blind. In the Ferguson years the player who would probably have had more touches in most given seasons would have been Paul Scholes.

Leicester won the league because they played a consistently high tempo, moved the ball forward quickly and suffered very few injuries. Under Diego Simeone, Atletico Madrid have become adept at conceding possession and then hitting back with hard, quick counter-attacks.

Whenever England go to major tournaments, they always seem to try to change their game – to attempt to play like the Dutch or the Spanish. And Holland and Spain are better at playing like Holland or Spain than we are. We do not seem to trust our own football instincts.

From the mid-1970s to the Heysel disaster, English clubs dominated European football. From 1999 to 2012 nine English teams reached a Champions League final and they largely did so because their opponents could not live with the tempo of football they played.

If you watch the 1999 semi-final between Juventus and Manchester United, you'll see how players of the quality of Zinedine Zidane and Edgar Davids struggle to contain the sheer force of United's play. The Premier League is not the best in the world and it has not been for years. But it always had drama and pace about it. The year Leicester became league champions, there was very little of either about.

# TWENTY-ONE

IS THERE AN ART OF MANAGEMENT, A POCKET BOOK YOU can pass from dug-out to dug-out? To me, the clue to management has always been in its name. It's about managing people – sometimes some very difficult people indeed.

When Pep Guardiola comes to Manchester City, he will face the most difficult management job of his career. When he took over at Barcelona, La Liga was a two-club league. By the time he became manager of Bayern Munich, the Bundesliga was fast on its way to becoming a one-club league. The Premier League will be full of obstacles of the kind he has not encountered before. It will be tougher, more competitive. There will be no winter break. He will find that the kinds of sides that in Spain or Germany rolled over for Barcelona and Bayern can bite back. He will also find himself in charge of some very difficult people.

At Barcelona, he would have been dealing with a team built around the products of the academy at La Masia; they were drilled to play in a certain way and to behave themselves off the pitch. He had no time for a maverick like Zlatan Ibrahimovic, who would turn up to training in a Ferrari rather than a club car.

Sometimes you have to bend a little, although how far you bend depends on how it plays out with the rest of the team. I gave Paul

McGrath a lot of leeway. At Aston Villa, our physio Jimmy Walker's job was to make sure that he did everything he could to make sure Paul played. What he did off the pitch was peripheral.

When Eric Cantona turned up to a reception in denim rather than the club blazer and tie everyone expected Alex Ferguson to go ballistic. Instead, Fergie said, 'That's Eric.'

When I took Manchester United on tour to Australia, I had to loan in a few players because we were short on numbers, so I brought in Frank Worthington. We were invited to an official reception where the dress code was 'smart casual'.

I told the players that slacks and a sweater would do. Frank came down in black leather trousers and a green armless T-shirt. I started to go over to remonstrate with him but someone said, 'That's what Frank considers to be smart casual.'

The best manager I have ever encountered during my time in football was Brian Clough. He took two clubs – Derby and Nottingham Forest – who had never won the league before to the league title. He very nearly took both of them to the European Cup.

I have used things I have picked up from almost every one of the great managers I've come across apart from Cloughie. Anyone who tried to would be lost because Brian Clough was a one-off, a genius. He had such an aura about him that it overcame everything.

Trevor Francis told me he would call a players' meeting and turn up an hour late. If you are a manager, the one thing you have to do when calling a players' meeting is turn up on time because, with every minute that goes by, the concentration level of the average footballer drops dramatically.

It was snowing outside and when Clough finally walked in, John Robertson made some kind of sarcastic comment and Brian turned to him and asked, 'Have you been feeding the birds this morning?' Robertson looked utterly nonplussed but Cloughie went on: 'Well, I have been feeding the birds because if I don't feed them, what will happen to them?'

Had I done that, I'd have been facing a riot, but that room full of

Nottingham Forest players stood there rapt. Several of Brian Clough's former players have gone into management and of those Martin O'Neill and Trevor Francis would have been the most successful, but I would be amazed if either man tried to be Brian Clough or imagined themselves as him.

Nobody now would dare call all of their team down to the hotel reception the night before a League Cup final, ply them with champagne and send them back to bed. Nobody would have the courage or have the licence to trust their instincts to that extent.

Don Revie did not trust his instincts – well, not to that degree. He put his trust in meticulous planning. One manager who should be recognised far more is Tony Collins, who in 1960 became the first black man to become a Football League manager when he took over at Rochdale; two years later he took them to the League Cup final.

When he left Rochdale he became Revie's chief scout at Leeds and he was my chief scout when I was at Manchester United. Tony idolised Revie and he once showed me one of the dossiers Revie had compiled on his opponents. There was page after page after page. It was like a book and I can't imagine any of his players would have got through it the night before a game. But they followed him to a man.

I remember talking to Terry Cooper about him and Terry sat back and sighed. 'I wish he would have let us off the leash a bit more. Leeds were a good enough side to have played with a lot more freedom than he allowed us.'

At Elland Road they always talked about the 7–0 thrashing they gave Southampton in 1972. It was an astonishing performance full of back-flicks and wonderful passing and they ought to have had the confidence to do it more often.

Had Leeds possessed a great striker, the team Don Revie built at Elland Road might have become the best club side in the history of English football, because they had everything else. They had Mick Jones and Allan Clarke but, if they'd had a Shearer, Leeds would have been unstoppable.

They suffered because they ended the season fighting on so many fronts. In 1973 they were in contention for the league, they were in the FA Cup final and the Cup Winners' Cup final and ended up with nothing. That summer, Revie told his players, 'We want the league and nothing else.' They won the title with something to spare.

Jose Mourinho has something of Clough and something of Revie in his make-up. He has that showmanship that Cloughie delighted in, but in terms of how he prepares his teams and the methods he uses, he is Revie.

I sometimes think of managers as golfers. Alex Ferguson is Jack Nicklaus, the man who has won more titles than anyone else. Bob Paisley is Tiger Woods for the sheer amount he won in a short space of time. Between 1976 and 1983, he won three European Cups, a UEFA Cup, six league titles and three League Cups. Brian Clough would be Seve Ballesteros. Someone once told me, 'You'd be Ernie Els.' The Big Easy.

Alan Curbishley once posed the question: 'How do you manage eleven millionaires?' I discount the money. I believe footballers are essentially the same as they have always been. One or two oddments aside, the vast majority of footballers respond to managers who they know, who they believe understand the game and whose orders they can trust. They want their training regime to be regular and they want the kind of discipline they can easily understand.

And managers change their personality over time. Alex Ferguson would not have allowed Eric Cantona the licence he did at the beginning of his time at Manchester United. It was only when Fergie was secure in his own position that he felt he could relax a bit more with someone like Cantona.

John Bond was someone I did take something from. When I was at Cambridge and he was at Norwich I used to drive to Norfolk just to watch him coach. In the same way, when I was manager of West Brom, I went up to Old Trafford just to watch Ossie Ardiles when he was playing for Tottenham. We couldn't afford to buy him, I just wanted to see him play. Andy Ritchie got a hat-trick for United but for me the highlight was Ardiles doing a back-heeled flick in the centre circle.

Bondy was a brilliantly innovative coach but he was more ambivalent about being a manager and the added responsibility that came with organising a club away from the training ground. But he was a great stimulus to me because he would always want to talk football.

Lawrie McMenemy was another. He had never played league football but Lawrie's strength was that he enjoyed working with big-name players. At Southampton, he signed Alan Ball, Kevin Keegan and Peter Shilton. Working with big names and big egos is an art and some managers don't relish it. Lawrie could manage people and he knew how to talk to and how to be himself around star footballers.

I used to love the camaraderie of the League Managers dinners in London and one evening a manager said to me, 'You employ footballers until they are no further use to you and then you eliminate them.' It sounded like a doctrine of the Corleone family to me.

The coaching courses at Lilleshall were the same. The courses themselves were fine but it would be in the bar afterwards where you would have the stimulus of intense conversations with people like Terry Venables, and John Lyall at West Ham, who was a very underrated football man and far harder than his public image. Jim Smith was another. With the rise of the foreign manager, I don't think that camaraderie exists in the way it used to.

From two o'clock to a quarter to three on a Saturday afternoon, most football managers will feel lonely and surplus to requirements. The team is out there on the pitch, warming up, and there is nothing much for you to do.

You end up just hanging around and when I was at Manchester United, my assistant Mick Brown would say, 'Just go in your office and come back at a quarter to three.' Otherwise, I would be tempted to make the kind of last-minute intervention that would usually involve telling a player something he had heard from me about four hundred times before.

So if Aston Villa were playing Manchester United at Villa Park I would ask Alex Ferguson if he wanted to come in for a cup of tea before the game. It is harder to talk to another manager after the game because there are now so many media commitments following the final whistle.

The first Premier League match at Highbury Arsene Wenger prepared for was against me, when I was in charge at Coventry. Although I don't hold with the idea that he revolutionised English football, he is to me the most significant manager of the Premier League era. What most Premier League managers do now is what Wenger was doing when he arrived at Arsenal in 1996.

The one criticism I would have of him is that, while all managers have a stubborn streak within them, he has been overly stubborn. Wenger has always enjoyed the backing of the Arsenal board, who run a club that is hugely profitable, and time and again he has passed up on the opportunity to bring high-quality reinforcements to the Emirates Stadium. From David Seaman's leaving of the club in 2003 to the arrival of Petr Cech a dozen years later, Arsenal did not have a goalkeeper who was the equal of their rivals.

Since the break-up of the wonderfully honed back four he inherited from George Graham, Arsenal's greatest weakness has been defensive. You thought when he appointed Steve Bould – who had been part of that defence – as his assistant things would change, but those cracks did not go away.

What makes Wenger special is that he prefers to create his own talent, rather than buy in the ready-made version as Jose Mourinho does. To him, the beauty of management lies in moulding his own footballers, of creating something from often very little.

Sometimes, when he has come near the title, I think he might have softened his principles a little, although I find the lack of respect he is shown by a section of Arsenal's supporters disgraceful. Were Arsene Wenger a businessman, he would win awards year after year.

If I were starting out today, would I manage the same way? If I found myself in the lower leagues, I would probably work as I did at Kettering and Cambridge, because scouting, looking at footballers and pounding the motorways into the small hours is still a central part of the job. The coaching would still be the same. The lower down the leagues you go, the harder you have to coach, because you have to work a lot more on repetition skills.

At the top end of the market you would have had to change because you now draw your players from so many markets, but at the heart of it all you would want your team to entertain. Not because I believe in entertaining for entertainment's sake but because I believe that the attacking game is the best way to win a football match.

There were times when I had to fight to play the passing game, in the years when what I called 'balloon ball' became popular and football became a kind of inverted rugby. Even Liverpool at their peak were not averse to it. Often when I was at Manchester United and we had them penned in, you would hear yells from their bench, usually directed to Phil Neal: 'Hit a few, hit it long.' Last season Leicester perfected a form of direct football that worked because it was played with pace and drive.

Football is a contest but it should be a contest that entertains. It is more than sixty years since I watched Ferenc Puskas and the rest of his Honved side train in the rain at Molineux. The game has changed but at its heart it remains the same. I can still hear the words of Jimmy Hogan, who coached Puskas and who was my coach when I was a kid at Aston Villa: 'If you've got the ball, you're attacking. If you haven't, you're defending.' Those principles haven't changed.

# INDEX